SpringerBriefs in Bu

MW00581043

More information about this series at http://www.springer.com/series/8860

Harald Dyckhoff · Rainer Souren

Performance Evaluation

Foundations and Challenges

 Springer

Harald Dyckhoff
School of Business and Economics
RWTH Aachen University
Rheine, Germany

Rainer Souren
Group of Sustainable Production
and Logistics Management
Ilmenau University of Technology
Ilmenau, Germany

ISSN 2191-5482   ISSN 2191-5490   (electronic)
SpringerBriefs in Business
ISBN 978-3-030-38731-0   ISBN 978-3-030-38732-7   (eBook)
https://doi.org/10.1007/978-3-030-38732-7

This Springer imprint is published by the registered company Springer Nature Switzerland AG
The registered company address is: Gewerbestrasse 11, 6330 Cham, Switzerland

Preface

Often, making the right decision is not easy. This does not only hold true for private life, e.g. when we buy a new, environmentally friendly car or book a holiday that should be as relaxing as possible. Entrepreneurial or political decisions also require comprehensive consideration of the objectives pursued and the existing alternatives against the backdrop of an uncertain environment. When planning future actions, decision makers can learn from past activities, if they succeed in evaluating them correctly. Therefore, adequate benchmarking primarily requires a goal-oriented evaluation of real past or realistic fictitious alternatives. But how can performance be evaluated without omitting important facts or exposing oneself to the danger of comparing 'apples and oranges'?

It is our firm conviction that, nowadays, important decisions can hardly be assessed solely on the basis of their financial effects. Non-financial performance evaluation is therefore becoming increasingly relevant; this holds especially true, when it is taken into consideration that almost every decision has ecological and social implications, too. Therefore, this book aims to provide a theoretical and conceptual basis for non-financial performance evaluation and to make the reader aware of the intelligent application of multi-criteria decision making. For this purpose, we develop a theoretical basic concept called Multi-Criteria Production Theory, which generalises and integrates theoretical components of decision and production theory, predominantly targeting efficiency measurement. It lays the foundations for various methods of non-financial valuation that are used in different scientific disciplines, the premises and limitations of which, however, are often not sufficiently explained. Primarily, these include Data Envelopment Analysis (DEA) and Life Cycle Assessment (LCA). The former is generalized in a separate chapter of this book in order to reveal pitfalls that are often looming during the application process. The latter is the core element of many environmental studies, which is why we believe it makes sense for the users of these methods to gain insights into decision-theoretical fundamentals and challenges which we discuss throughout the entire book and predominantly in the concluding chapter.

This book brings together the results achieved by the first author in the course of many years of research in the field of performance measurement. It includes a large vi

number of findings; some originate, in terms of contents, and to some extent even word for word, from earlier contributions to various journals. In order to make the origins as traceable as possible and in order to provide a hint for further reading, these particularly relevant contributions are explicitly mentioned at the beginning of each chapter. Nonetheless, this book is not merely a summary of earlier findings, but it provides, on the one hand, a systematic theoretical concept, and on the other hand, a comprehensive overview of the concept including numerous examples, which, for didactic reasons, have been kept simple.

Such a book is never solely the work of its authors, but it also contains a considerable number of ideas and suggestions of other scientists with whom the authors have collaborated in recent years. Therefore, first of all, our thanks go to all the co-authors of the contributions the contents of which have been included into this work. Furthermore, we have received suggestions from several colleagues, co-workers and friends – a classification that is by no means disjunct – who have read the book through, critically. Many thanks to all of you! Pars pro toto, we would like to point out one person in particular, without whom the book would probably never have been published in the present version: With her own professional, warm-hearted and, in spite of the constant requests for changes, never despairing manner, Sigrun Leipe had a significant impact on the visual design of the book. Thanks a million!

Harald Dyckhoff   Rainer Souren
Aachen   Ilmenau

November 2019

Contents

Chapter 1
Main Performance Categories: Effectiveness and Efficiency[1]

Abstract.   Traditional methods of cost/benefit-analysis in economics and of management accounting in business administration usually measure the performance of activities in monetary terms. In contrast, this book focuses on particular aspects of the theory, methodology, and application of performance evaluations for non-financial data. They are relevant for a wide range of application areas where other values than purely market-based economic ones are important, e.g. because of social or ecological impacts in cases of sustainability evaluations. The first chapter explains why the measurement of effectiveness and efficiency forms the core of performance evaluations in general. Based on Max Weber's concept of purposive rationality, it approaches performance evaluation as a kind of generalised cost/benefit-analysis for non-financial types of costs and benefits which measure the disadvantages and advantages of an action on distinct, incommensurable scales. The approach is based both on decision theory and production theory. In this way, well-known concepts and methods of performance measurement, such as those of data envelopment analysis or life cycle assessment, are enhanced by a sound foundation for fruitful and valid empirical research and applications. In addition, the scope, focus, and contents of the following chapters are sketched.

Keywords   Benefits • Costs • Effectiveness • Efficiency • Key performance indicator • Performance measurement • Rationality

---

[1] Section 1.2.1 is essentially based on and translated from Dyckhoff and Ahn (2010) by permission of Springer Nature.

1.1   Rationale of (Non-financial) Performance Evaluation

About 100 years ago, the well-known sociologist Max Weber wrote:[2]

> Action is rationally oriented to a system of discrete individual ends when the ends, the means, and the secondary results are all rationally taken into account and weighted. This involves rational consideration of alternative means to the ends, of the relations of the ends to other prospective results of employment of any given means, and finally of the relative importance of different possible ends.

Thus, ends, means and secondary results compose three different classes of criteria determining the rationality of an action or of an actor. In the above quotation, the term 'ends' is used to name the purposes which constitute the original motives for the action considered in the situation at hand. The extent to which these main ends are achieved determines the *effectiveness* (or *effectivity*) of an action, while the consideration of the ends in relation to the means as well as to the secondary results appraises its *efficiency*. These notions are meant by the following phrases known from business practice: "Do the right things!" (be effective) and "Do things right!" (be efficient).

Example 1.1: Buying versus shopping

Assume a decision maker's single end is to buy a new shirt of good quality. She wants to spend as little time as possible for the searching and buying process while the price of the shirt is of no importance (within given limits). Then, her effectiveness is described by the answer to the question how much the shirt bought comes up to the intended quality. Her efficiency may be measured by the minutes or hours needed in relation to the quality of the shirt.

Now consider a second decision maker whose main end is also to purchase a new shirt of good quality. He considers the price to be payed as an undesirable outcome of the searching and buying process. Furthermore, time is of no importance (within given limits); on the contrary, he likes to walk through the shops to have a look and to try on different shirts. His effectiveness can be described in the same way as for the first decision maker, as long as the shopping process itself forms a secondary result only. But, in order to evaluate the efficiency of his action, this desirable effect of browsing in a shop has to be taken into account in addition to weighing up the price of the shirt and its quality.

If the rationality of an action is evaluated, effectiveness and efficiency form the two main categories of analysis regarding the quality of the decision to carry out the

---

[2] Cf. the translation from Weber et al. (1964). Here, the term 'ends' is used in plural referring to Weber's (1921/1980, p. 21) original definition: "Zweckrational handelt, wer sein Handeln nach Zweck, Mitteln und Nebenfolgen orientiert und dabei sowohl die Mittel gegen die Zwecke, wie die Zwecke gegen die Nebenfolgen, wie endlich auch die verschiedenen möglichen Zwecke gegeneinander rational abwägt."

action. Such an analysis may be called ***performance evaluation*** according to the pertinent literature on performance measurement. The following definition of the last notion, originating from Neely et al. (1995, p. 80), is widely used: "***Performance measurement*** can be defined as the process of quantifying the efficiency and effectiveness of action." Performance evaluation comprises data from (exact) measurement, and in addition considers qualitative aspects of effectiveness and efficiency if they are relevant.[3] Moreover, there may be further categories of rationality, e.g. the *legitimacy* or the *sustainability* of actions. Often, such categories characterise a kind of ***value rationality*** ("Wertrationalität") which Max Weber distinguishes from the above ***purposive rationality*** ("Zweckrationalität").

Literature on rational action usually neglects the secondary results in such a way that only the relation of means to the ends is analysed. The achievement of an end is valued as a *benefit*, the employment of a means usually as a *cost*. A characteristic feature of performance measurement and evaluation is that often these benefits and costs cannot be measured in financial terms and are moreover incommensurable *a priori*. This holds especially true, when secondary results of an action are taken into account. Such results are mostly undesirable, like e.g. waste or emissions of production and consumption. They may, however, also be desirable, like e.g. an unintended discovery or invention made during an exploration. Thus, secondary results represent certain types of – usually incommensurable – costs or benefits, too.

In this book, a ***benefit*** or ***cost*** of an action is defined as a certain type of desirable and undesirable result, respectively. Thus, by definition, minimum costs and maximum benefits are preferred. In this view, Max Weber's notion of purposively rational action aims to find a balance between the maximisation of the benefits and the minimisation of the costs. As a rule, the intended multiple ends as well as the unintended desirable secondary results represent different types of benefits, and the applied multiple means as well as the undesirable secondary results represent respective types of costs.[4] Therefore, the performance evaluation of actions can also be regarded as a generalisation of the well-known (monetary) *cost/benefit-analysis* in comparison to non-monetary valuations (Dyckhoff and Ahn 2002). Thus, it constitutes a kind of *multi-criteria decision analysis* or *assessment*, in which the performance criteria are determined by the different types of costs and benefits. ***Non-financial performance evaluation***, in particular, is characterised by the fact that at least one relevant performance criterion cannot be measured in such (e.g. monetary) terms that it can be easily aggregated alongside with the other relevant criteria into a single measure of overall performance.

---

[3] Performance evaluation is thus part of *management accounting* which "is the process of measuring, analyzing, and reporting financial and non-financial information that helps managers make decisions to fulfil the goals of an organization" (Datar and Rajan 2018, p. 22).

[4] However, means of production whose consumption or destruction is desired, such as scrap tyres in cement production, represent an exception from this rule (cf. Example 2.1 in Sect. 2.1.2).

1.2   Particular Aspects of Performance Evaluation

The present book focuses on certain fundamental aspects of non-financial performance evaluation in regard to quantitative data. First of all, we concentrate on some
specific, nevertheless fairly general theories and methods of performance evaluation
which are relevant for a broad variety of applications in practice. Furthermore, we
assume deterministic data. Though, for most of the topics dealt with, extensions or
similar approaches exist which allow to handle uncertain data. Many of the concepts
and assertions of the book are of general importance for such stochastic extensions
or approaches, too.

1.2.1   Basics and Theoretical Foundations

Most evaluation methods – like e.g. those of cost accounting in business administration, data envelopment analysis (DEA) for efficiency measurement or life cycle assessment (LCA) in environmental management – are both a tool for empirical research on the performance of human behaviour and an artefact that can be used to
improve performance itself. Hence, they are part of behavioural science as well as
of design science, each with a different paradigm. The first has its roots in natural
science research and seeks to develop and justify theories (i.e. principles and laws)
explaining or predicting organisational or human phenomena, while the second has
its roots in engineering as well as the arts, seeking to create useful innovative artefacts (in a broad sense: ideas, practices, techniques, products). "Such artefacts are
not exempt from natural laws or behavioural theories", Hevner et al. (2004, p. 76)
state in their presentation of a concise conceptual framework and clear guidelines
for design science (of information systems), and they continue: "To the contrary,
their creation relies on existing *kernel theories* that are applied, tested, modified,
and extended through the experience, creativity, intuition, and problem solving ca-
pabilities of the researcher." In this sense, we will look for such a kernel theory of
(non-financial) performance evaluation.

Since performance evaluation is a kind of multi-criteria decision analysis, it will
make sense to base our approach on decision theory. Accordingly, an ***action*** (or
activity) is characterised as the process between the decision maker's subject system
and the object system in which the action is executed (Bamberg et al. 2012, pp. 1ff.).
The decision field can be formalised by the following elements:

- activity set (also option set or set of alternatives) $\mathcal{A}$ as the compilation of all
  activities a that can be executed by the decision maker
- situation set $\mathcal{S}$ as the compilation of possible scenarios s

- result function $r(a; s)$ that indicates the consequences resulting from the alternative $a \in \mathcal{A}$ in situation $s \in \mathcal{S}$.

Example 1.2: Travelling from Basel to Cologne

Several options $a \in \mathcal{A}$ to travel along the river Rhine from Basel in Switzerland to Cologne in Germany shall be evaluated regarding their performance with respect to certain criteria: Flying by helicopter or alternatively by a regular airliner from Basel to Cologne-Bonn airport combined with taxicab transports between the airports and the cities; driving a Porsche on the autobahn or an electric car, riding a motorbike or a bicycle through the rolling hills of the Black Forrest and the vineyards along the Rhine; travelling by railway or by ship on the Rhine itself. The level of detail necessary for the description of the individual options a and what kinds of results $r(a; s)$ have to be considered depend on the objectives that define the performance criteria of the evaluation. If, e.g., the actual objective is to get to a conference in Cologne in time, effectiveness of the different options is described only by the arrival time as the decisive result. Efficiency can then be based on criteria such as travel expenses, duration or comfort. If, in contrast, the journey is a vacation trip, effectiveness is more likely fulfilled when it is beautiful and relaxing, while the trip's duration could have a different, even perhaps opposite impact on efficiency. Ecological objectives may play an important role instead. Uncertain scenarios $s \in \mathcal{S}$ affect the results $r(a; s)$, such as the weather conditions while cycling or travelling by boat with regard to well-being or comfort.

Usually, the alternatives $a \in \mathcal{A}$ are not described in detail, but only briefly denominated for clear identification. Instead, their results $r(a; s)$ have to include all the information necessary for the valuation regarding the relevant types of costs and benefits $v = (c; b)$, defined by the ends, means and secondary results. From a mathematical point of view, these evaluations represent a function (or mapping) of the relevant alternative results on costs and benefits: $v = v(r) = v(r(a; s))$. However, this does not necessarily implicate quantification, neither of the results r nor of the performance values v. Both can generally be described in any kind, i.e. not only formally but also purely verbally. In contrast, performance *measurement* requires a kind of quantification of costs and benefits $v = (c; b)$.

In this book, we particularly understand the decision maker as a *producer* who controls the process of employment of the means applied in order to achieve the intended ends. This allows us to make use of particular rationality concepts and findings of *production theory* additionally to those of decision theory. Thus, the kernel theory of this book can be named ***decision-based production theory***.

Furthermore, since we concentrate on decisions under certainty, situation set $\mathcal{S}$ consists of only one element and is therefore ignored in the following. The emphasis is on the activity set $\mathcal{A}$. It is called ***production possibility set*** (PPS) here, specified by the symbol $\mathcal{P} = \mathcal{A}$. The PPS forms a subset of the technology $\mathcal{T}$ which comprises all activities that are feasible in principle on the basis of the available knowledge and transformation processes for value creation. In reality, however, the decision space is situationally restricted by the so-called restriction space $\mathcal{R}$. Therefore, the feasible actions result from the intersection $\mathcal{P} = \mathcal{T} \cap \mathcal{R}$ of the activities that are technologically feasible and satisfy the restrictions (Dyckhoff 1992, p. 86; 2006, p. 64).

Production is a process of transforming input into output to generate a value (Dyckhoff 2006, p. 3). For the purpose of performance evaluation, each production activity a can usually be described bijectively and completely by the relevant process-specific *input quantities* x and *output quantities* y. Thus, each activity can be identified by the representation $z := (x; y)$ of the related inputs and outputs: $a \equiv z$. Therefore, usually, there is no further distinction between the activity and the description of its inputs and outputs.

Remark: If there is no bijection, input and output are at least uniquely determined by the activity, which can be symbolised by an index: $z_a = (x_a; y_a)$. However, bijection does not represent a strong limitation of generality. Either several alternatives with identical input/output-description can be considered as equal without further differentiation necessary, or the possibly relevant discriminating properties can be integrated into the inputs and outputs. Depending on how the terms 'input' and 'output' are precisely defined, other pieces of alternative-specific information can be important, e.g. process variables for temperature and pressure. In contrast, this book is based on the usual definition of input and output – presented in Section 2.1.1 and commonly used in production theory – that excludes such additional activity specific data.

A priori, it is not obvious by what kinds of inputs and outputs an activity is described exactly enough. Ultimately, this depends on the purpose of the description. In the context of performance evaluation, all kinds of inputs and outputs are relevant that contain *all those pieces of information that are necessary for the evaluation and specific for the respective activity*. Input x and output y must therefore reflect the means used and the ends achieved as well as secondary results insofar as they are relevant with regard to the objectives of the decision maker.[5]

Remark: Frisch (1965, p. 14) concludes with respect to the countless number of things which are part of a production process or influence it: "No analysis, however completely it is carried out, can include all these things at once. In undertaking a production analysis we must therefore select certain factors whose effect we wish to consider more closely." The selection depends on the specific purpose of the model as well as on the particular view of the model designer. Therefore, production models always build partial pictures of real production processes, only, and corresponding performance analyses of production systems measure those aspects at most which are relevant for the evaluation of the creation or destruction of those values determined by the decision maker, evaluator or model designer. Thus, in general, many more performance criteria are relevant for sustainability performance evaluations than in purely economically motivated analyses.

---

[5] From a decision-theoretic point of view, not only the output but also the input (provided or used) is the result or consequence of the decision for a specific production activity. This corresponds with the *identity principle* of cost accounting (Riebel 1994), whereupon each cost and benefit must be attributed to the decision that has triggered them.

If, e.g., climate protection is a relevant objective, this must be reflected in the activity's description, particularly by capturing the emissions of climate-relevant gases (carbon dioxide, methane etc.). From a production-theoretical perspective, emissions are a kind of output in any case. In terms of climate protection, however, the emission of greenhouse gases is harmful; it generates an undesirable secondary result that should be avoided as far as possible. Instead of directly assessing an activity on the basis of its inputs and outputs, *decision-based production theory* assesses its consequences on the basis of the producer's or any other decision maker's preferences (Dyckhoff and Spengler 2010). In contrast, traditional production theory usually deals with the special case solely, in which the preference relation is explicitly determined via the Pareto-Koopmans dominance principle, according to which less input or more output are preferred for each object type *ceteris paribus*. However, it generally depends on the relevant objectives, how input and output have actually to be assessed and what types of inputs and outputs have to be analysed at all. They can be derived by suitable decision-theoretical procedures of generating and structuring objectives (Eisenführ et al. 2010, Chap. 3).

Usually, with regard to the objectives, the decision maker or evaluator does not only need to know the inputs and outputs specific for the individual activities, but he or she often needs to take into consideration further general data about the decision situation which are identical for all activities of the PPS. These include, e.g., market prices for inputs and outputs which are required to calculate the profit or carbon dioxide equivalency factors for different greenhouse gases when calculating the emissions' climate impact. Hence, such data are represented in the results $r(x; y)$, that thus also capture the impacts on the environment of the production system as decision field.

Decision theory generally assumes that each alternative can be valued by its results solely. Accordingly, we assume that the processes that have to be evaluated are described sufficiently in-depth by their inputs and outputs and that no further information about the particular process is needed. However, further information on the decision maker's preferences and corresponding data is necessary. The *costs* and *benefits* as the performance measures $v = (c; b)$ of an activity $z = (x; y)$ therefore arise out of its results $r(z)$, complemented by all further relevant data from the decision field: $v = v(r) = v(r(z))$. Thus defined, costs and benefits represent the advantages and disadvantages of a decision for a certain activity valued by selected multiple performance measures.[6]

---

[6] The use of these terms is similar to the *conception I* of management accounting by Ewert and Wagenhofer (2014, p. 35). They also deduce them from the basic model of decision theory as negative and positive consequences of a decision and call them *costs I* ("Kosten I") and *benefits I* ("Leistungen I").

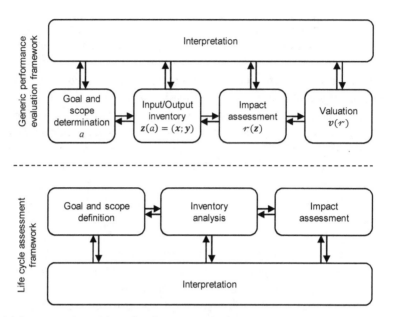

Fig. 1.1 Structure and procedure of performance evaluation

Figure 1.1 (upper part) outlines the basic structure and procedure of performance evaluation. The evaluation of an activity a can be understood as a ***recursive, interdependent, four-step process***. In the first step, the evaluation's subject and objectives as well as the decision field are specified (*goal and scope determination*). Then, with respect to the selected objectives, the alternative-specific inputs and outputs $z(a) = (x; y)$ are determined (*input/output inventory*). Based on that, all relevant results or impacts $r = r(z)$ are assessed (*impact assessment*), which are finally valued by performance measures $v(r)$ (*valuation*). The decision maker or an (external) evaluator is responsible for the *interpretation* of the results in each step. This procedure is generic for non-financial performance evaluation and can be found in similar form in different application areas, such as LCA; its framework is visualised in Figure 1.1 (lower part) – rotated by 90° compared to its usual presentation for better comparability (EN ISO 14040:2006). In LCA, however, the valuation, deliberately explicated in our framework, usually is part of the interpretation.[7]

It should be noted that such a performance evaluation procedure must include several feedback loops consisting of suitable interpretations to ensure that all inputs and outputs as well as their impacts which are relevant to the objectives and the alternatives are chosen appropriately.

---

[7] Occasionally, the importance of valuation for Life Cycle (Sustainability) Assessment is emphasised similarly to our approach by including a separate fourth step. Thies et al. (2019, Fig. 1) name that step 'evaluation', while we use the term in a broader sense and thus prefer 'valuation'.

In simple cases, the evaluation can start directly with the inputs and outputs, so that the third step, the impact analysis, is not necessarily explicit, but can be integrated into the valuation step or might be even totally omitted: $v = v(z)$. For the sake of simplicity, but without essentially limiting generality, we will assume this case in the theoretically and methodologically oriented Chapters 2 and 3.

In non-financial performance evaluation practice, the distinction between the impact analysis in step three – using intersubjective data as far as possible – and the valuation in step four – that cannot be conducted without subjective preferences – is of utmost importance for the transparency and validity of the whole process. Therefore, even impacts and values themselves are often determined in a multistage procedure, e.g. in the eco-efficiency method of BASF[8]. This method is well established in the LCA practice (Dyckhoff et al. 2015). Figure 1.2 shows its hierarchical disaggregation of the total ecological impact. Here, various ecological impacts are used as performance criteria; they are categorised into three input- and three output-related criteria, whereby those caused by the emissions have to be aggregated within two prior steps on lower impact assessment and valuation levels. Hierarchies of performance indicators will be a further focal point of this book (Sect. 3.4, 4.3 and 4.4).

As mentioned before, inputs and outputs, results as well as costs and benefits may in general be described in different forms, e.g. also just verbally. Therefore, their formal, mathematical representation by multidimensional vectors leads to a

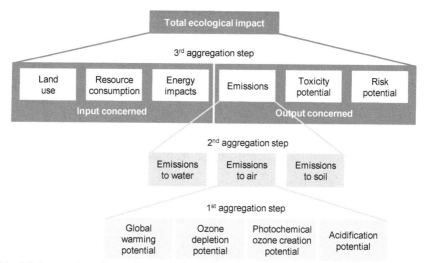

Fig. 1.2 Aggregation scheme of ecological criteria (cf. Dyckhoff et al. 2015, p. 1560)

---

[8] The method has been extended by BASF to include social impacts; this extension is called SEE-BALANCE® (Uhlman and Saling 2017).

limitation of measurable aspects and should be clearly regarded as an assumption of an intended performance analysis.[9] Traditional production theory is usually limited to this particular case. Then, the production possibility set $\mathcal{P}$ covers the de facto feasible production activities as vectors $z = (x; y)$ in a multidimensional space of real numbers, the dimensions of which are usually defined by the *different types of inputs and outputs*. That also holds true for the production theory presented in this book. The results $r(z)$ and the values $v(r)$, however, are defined in their own appropriate multidimensional number spaces. In order to model and analyse them, almost all well-known methods of decision theory can be used, particularly those of multi-criteria decision making (MCDM) and multi-attribute utility theory (MAUT). In Chapter 2 of this book, ***multi-criteria production theory*** (MCPT) is developed as a particular instance of a decision-based production theory and is used as a theoretical basis for performance analysis and its applications thereafter.

1.2.2 Concepts and Methods

A wide range of concepts and methods can be considered for performance evaluation. We focus on those that are covered by the decision-based production theory outlined in the last section. They can be differentiated according to how strongly they aggregate the performance values.[10] At the lowest level, the information that is relevant for each activity's performance is described by its specific inputs and outputs $z = (x; y)$ as well as by the interrelated results $r(z)$ that are objectively or intersubjectively determinable. Then, on higher levels, the evaluation proceeds by using appropriate performance measures that condense the valuation further and further, thus allowing for a better comparison of the activities with regard to their preferability. Then, at upper levels, the performance is represented by a few ***key performance indicators*** (***KPI***) only, or in extreme cases by a single measure as a one-dimensional top KPI. The intermediate levels can contain various kinds of multidimensional valuations based on preference-based indicators that include the respective costs and benefits of an activity: $(c; b) = \tilde{v}(x; y) = v(r(x; y))$.

Example 1.3: Economic performance of four factories
Four similar factories $j = 1, \ldots, 4$ belonging to one and the same company will be evaluated by their top management regarding their (relative) performance. In a first approach, a purely economic point of view is applied. Only two production

---

[9] As mentioned before, performance measurement is characterised by this assumption, whereas performance evaluation can also consider qualitative values.
[10] Examples of different hierarchies of performance aggregation for various approaches to an environmentally oriented production theory are shown by Dyckhoff (2003).

factors (x_{1j}, x_{2j}), e.g. labour and capital, are considered as relevant cost types apart from the benefit from selling the product y_{1j}. The four production activities $z_j = (x_{1j}, x_{2j}; y_{1j})$ observed in the past year are $z_1 = (1, 5; 1)$, $z_2 = (10, 2; 2)$, $z_3 = (12, 12; 3)$ and $z_4 = (20, 16; 4)$. Since factory 4 was able to reach an output of four units of the product it is *most effective* if the company's current main objective is market leadership – at least in case that the sizes of the four factories' markets are roughly the same.

The management also wants to compare the factories' efficiency in order to obtain some *benchmarks* which might help the less productive factories to learn from *best practice*, the result of which might lead to corresponding improvements. As the factories in question are located in four different countries, each with its own currency, the factor prices cannot be compared easily. Instead, the *factor intensities* will be used as performance indicators for comparison, i.e. $v_j = (v_{1j}, v_{2j}) = (x_{1j}/y_{1j}, x_{2j}/y_{1j})$, which results in: $v_1 = (1, 5)$, $v_2 = (5, 1)$, $v_3 = (4, 4)$ and $v_4 = (5, 4)$. Hence, factory 4 is more labour intensive than factory 3 ($5 > 4$) while their capital intensities are equal ($4 = 4$). Regarding the other three factories, however, their factor intensities vary such that none of them is better or equal compared to the intensities of the other two factories.

In order to enable a less effective or less efficient factory to improve its operations by learning from best practice, it is a necessary prerequisite that an adequate modification of its previous activity is possible at all. That is, the new activity to be executed must also be an element of the PPS of the respective factory. Even if all four factories possess the same technology $\mathcal{T}$, in the end, their country-specific restrictions $\mathcal{R}_j$ may not be identical. Otherwise – if all four PPSs are identical, i.e. $\mathcal{P}_j = \mathcal{T} \cap \mathcal{R}$ –, the other factories can become more effective by copying the operations of factory 4 from the past year, nevertheless at the cost of less *productivity* of one or both production factors. But, if a further activity is possible, namely $z_5 = (16, 16; 4) \in \mathcal{P}$, factory 3 can become more effective without harming its productivity, when it increases all inputs and outputs by one third, and factory 4 can become more efficient without reducing its effectiveness by eliminating four units of its labour input. A sufficient condition for $z_5 = (16, 16; 4) \in \mathcal{P}$ are *constant returns to scale* of the technology together with *identical factor availabilities*. Then, $z_3 = (12, 12; 3) \in \mathcal{P}$ and $z_4 = (20, 16; 4) \in \mathcal{P}$ imply $z_5 = (16, 16; 4) \in \mathcal{P}$.

In case of an *additive* technology, from the production activities $z_1 = (1, 5; 1) \in \mathcal{P}$ and $z_2 = (10, 2; 2) \in \mathcal{P}$ of the past year follows that also $z_6 = (11, 7; 3) \in \mathcal{P}$. This new activity, a combination of the observed operations of factories 1 and 2, is feasible and dominates activity $z_3 = (12, 12; 3)$ because it uses less input of both production factors for the same output. Furthermore, the additive combination of the observed activities z_1 and z_3 dominates activity

z_4. On the other hand, the observed activities of factories 1 and 2 are not domi-nated, not even in cases of linear technologies (which are additive with constant returns to scale; cf. e.g. Dyckhoff 2006, p. 63). Under such circumstances, fac-tories 1 and 2 are best performers regarding efficiency, and both can also become more effective by proportionally increasing their inputs and outputs as far as enough labour and capital (and possibly other factors like e.g. natural resources) are available.

For a further comparison of activities z_1 and z_2, more information is nec-essary which allows a stronger valuation. For example, if the company sets in-ternal prices for the two factors and the product, this would allow to calculate the profit, the contribution margin or the product costs as one-dimensional (key) performance indicators for the activities observed.

The example shows how a performance evaluation of activities can be conducted solely with respect to the data of the inputs and outputs, i.e. without any information of prices or other weighting factors that would allow to calculate a trade-off between them. However, some prerequisites are indispensable. In the above example, the central assumption is that the decision maker *ceteris paribus* prefers less input and more output.[11] Thus, according to our definition, each input represents a certain kind of non-financial cost as well as each output a non-financial benefit.

Often, however, an efficiency comparison of the activities observed is only pos-sible when assumptions about the underlying PPS are valid. As Example 1.3 shows, additional fictitious activities can be constructed that dominate some of the individ-ual activities observed. A ***dominance relation*** occurs when these fictitious activities lead to improvements for at least one input or output without impairing other inputs and outputs. The assumptions regarding the construction of additional activities re-late to the properties of the technology (as set of all activities in principle realisable) as well as to the actual restrictions. The stronger the assumptions about the techno-logical properties the bigger the number of activities available for a comparison of performance. The data of the activities observed are supplemented by these ficti-tious activities, whereby the resulting PPS often envelops the activities observed. The associated method is therefore known as ***data envelopment analysis (DEA)***, which is a main focus of this book (Chap. 3).

As long as the assumptions on the properties of the PPS are realistic, DEA de-termines fictitious, but feasible activities that can serve as *benchmarks* for a ***deci-sion-making unit*** (DMU) which is responsible for an inefficient activity. In addition to this recommendation, DEA calculates one-dimensional (in)efficiency scores of the activities observed or the related DMU. Usually, this happens by determining

---

[11] This preference assumption only holds true for the implied case that solely goods are consid-ered. The preference direction has to be reversed for bads (cf. Example 1.6 and in general assump-tion A6b in Sect. 2.2.1).

the distance from an inefficient activity to another one dominating it, applying a selected metric for the multidimensional number space considered. However, the selection of this metric is also based on additional assumptions, in this case concerning the decision maker's values (Kleine 2004).

Example 1.4 (1.3 continued): Additive input efficiency of factories
The distance between activity $z_3 = (12, 12; 3)$ and $z_6 = (11, 7; 3)$ in Example 1.3 can be measured using the so called 'City block'-metric as the equally weighted sum of the possible percentage reduction of both inputs, i.e. $0.5 \cdot (12 - 11)/12 + 0.5 \cdot (12 - 7)/12 = 0.25$. The inefficiency of $z_3 = (12, 12; 3)$ relative to $z_6 = (11, 7; 3)$ would then be $1 - 0.25 = 0.75$. This means that both inputs can be reduced *on average* to 75 % of their actual value.

With such *additive slack-based* models, DEA usually uses input and output weights derived from the data observed to avoid subjective determination (cf. Sect. 3.2.2). Due to the weighting problems, DEA rather uses *radial* models that only measure proportional improvements, either for the inputs or the outputs, and therefore correspond to a 'Chebychev'-metric (cf. Sect. 3.2.1).

Example 1.5 (1.3 and 1.4 continued): Radial input efficiency of factories
The *input-oriented* radial distance between the two activities $z_3 = (12, 12; 3)$ and $z_6 = (11, 7; 3)$, without increasing the output, is one unit for both inputs, while the input capital on its own could be further reduced by four units. The radial input-oriented inefficiency of $z_3 = (12, 12; 3)$ relative to $z_6 = (11, 7; 3)$ is usually measured with the percentage $11/12 = 91.67$ %, to which, at best, both inputs can be reduced *simultaneously* and *proportionally*.

Thus, radial performance measures often capture efficiency only to some extent, in Example 1.5 as a weak input-efficiency, while ignoring further improvements for individual inputs or outputs. Should a performance measurement be conducted by using solely a single indicator, there is always a risk that the performance evaluation ignores important aspects.

Nevertheless, valuations based on a single performance indicator are common practice. Such a top key performance indicator is intended to measure the overall performance for the activity observed according to its **success** as one-dimensional benefit. In purely economic performance evaluations based on monetary values, the company's *profit* or *shareholder value* regularly represents its success. In purely ecological evaluations, the *total ecological impact* of a product, of a technical procedure or of any defined physical system, clearly demarcated from its environment by a system boundary, is such a single performance indicator. The eco-efficiency method of BASF (dealt with in Sect. 4.3) considers this total ecological impact as one of two (negatively valued) KPIs (cf. Fig. 1.2). The second KPI is the total economic life cycle cost.

Example 1.6 (1.3 – 1.5 continued): Eco-efficiency of four factories

At the end of Example 1.3, we already stated that more information allowing for a stronger valuation is necessary for a progressing comparison of activities z_1 and z_2, e.g. information about existing market prices for the inputs and outputs. Now assume that prices for both factors and for the product are given with 4, 5, and 100 units of the same currency (CU) per quantity unit (QU) of input or output, respectively. Then, the profits achieved by last year's activities of the four factories are 71 CU for z_1, 150 CU for z_2, 192 CU for z_3, and 240 CU for z_4, while the respective margins of the product are 71, 75, 64, and 60 CU/QU. Thus, factory 4 is best regarding total profit, and factory 2 is best regarding profit margins, if they are solely compared with the other three factories respectively. In the course of learning from best practice, however, such a comparison requires an adequate underlying PPS, for example one with constant returns to scale within the relevant scale interval. Without this prerequisite, the maximum profit of 240 CU for factory 4 cannot be achieved by the others, and factories 1, 3 and 4 cannot adapt the production of factory 2 with its minimal product unit costs of 25 CU/QU.

Let us furthermore assume that the performances of the four factories are not only to be evaluated from an economic but also from an ecological point of view. Apart from profit maximisation, the second main objective is the minimisation of climate impact. Here, climate impact results from the emissions (y_{2j}, y_{3j}) of the two greenhouse gases carbon dioxide (CO_2) and methane (CH_4) that complement each activity vector. The respective emissions from the past year are (12, 2) for factory 1, (10, 6) for factory 2, (22, 5) for factory 3 and (25, 7) for factory 4. These quantities are displayed in Figure 1.3 (on the left) in a *cobweb diagram* together with the quantities of the two inputs and the product output. To allow a faster interpretation of the graph the scales of the different inputs and outputs are plotted with the direction of their desirability towards outside. As all four zigzag lines intersect, none of the original four activities dominates another one – at least if only the four factories are compared separately with each other.

In case of an additive PPS (cf. Example 1.3), the added production of factories 1 and 2 of the past year must be a possible activity, i.e. $z_6 = (11, 7; 3, 22, 8) \in \mathcal{P}$. Due to its larger emissions, this activity does no longer dominate the production of the past year of factory 3 which results in $z_3 = (12, 12; 3, 22, 5)$. Thus, while both activities produce 3 QU of the product, the first one (z_6) dominates the second one (z_3) economically: (11, 7) < (12, 12), but is dominated ecologically: (22, 8) > (22, 5).

Since the emission of one mass unit of methane has a climate impact within 100 years (*radiative forcing*) which is 28 times higher than that of carbon dioxide, both greenhouse gases have a negative ecological performance calculated by $c_j = r_j = y_{2j} + 28y_{3j}$. This results in climate impacts, which are measured

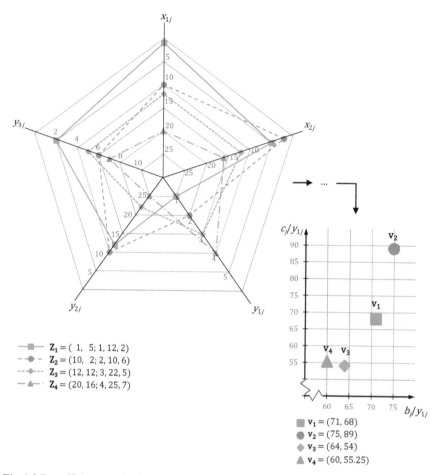

Fig. 1.3 Eco-efficiency evaluation of four factories

by 'carbon dioxide equivalents', of 68 QU for factory 1, 178 QU for factory 2, 162 QU for factory 3 and 221 QU for factory 4. Thus, factory 1 is most effective concerning the total climate effect. In case of a PPS with constant returns to scale, it makes sense to compare the factories' climate impact per product unit. If the profit and the climate impact of factory j are denoted by b_j as benefit and c_j as cost, one obtains the following margins $v_j = (b_j/y_{1j}, c_j/y_{1j})$, that are displayed in Figure 1.3 (diagram on the right): (71, 68) for factory 1, (75, 89) for factory 2, (64, 54) for factory 3 and (60, 55.25) for factory 4. Thus, regarding profit and climate change per product unit, factory 3 dominates factory 4 (64 > 60 and 54 < 55.25) although its unit emissions of carbon dioxide are higher (22/3 > 25/4).

The example shows that a change of the PPS or of the objectives may also change the performance evaluation of an activity. It furthermore indicates that the more the inputs and outputs are consistently aggregated by performance measures, the more activities are dominated by others. In this book, these observations and more assertions will be analysed and proven as general propositions (particularly in Chap. 2 and 3).

1.2.3   Practical Aspects

In practice, performance evaluation has to face several facts that often do not coincide with the assumptions underlying the methods used. Problems that may arise in this context will also be discussed in some parts of this book (particularly in Chap. 4). As decision-oriented production theory is our kernel theory, we concentrate on such aspects which apply to the intersection of production theory and decision theory. In particular, we consider those aspects which refer to the dependence of performance indicators on different valuation levels, such as nonlinear value functions, the rationality of weighting procedures, the construction of key performance indicators or the lacking knowledge of quantitative relations. Thereby, we focus on methods which evaluate the performance of those kinds of activities that are essentially characterised by the transformation of inputs into outputs.

1.3   Scope, Focus, and Contents of the Book

The previous examples have indicated that *(non-financial) performance evaluation* is a task which arises in most areas of human life. Therefore, the topics of this book are of importance for many scientific disciplines which are confronted with the problem of carving out and assessing the advantages and disadvantages of certain actions that arise in connection with the production and consumption of goods and services. As already remarked before, this book focuses on cases of deterministic non-financial performance data and concentrates on some specific, quantitatively oriented, nevertheless fairly general foundations and methods which are relevant for a whole variety of applications in practice. Apart from this introductory chapter, the text is structured into three further chapters which cover *theory*, *methods* and *challenges* of non-financial performance evaluation as main topics.

In *Chapter 2*, a generalisation of traditional production theories, called *multi-criteria production theory* (MCPT) is developed. Furthermore, main theorems of

MCPT are proven and the fundamentality of some axioms otherwise used in traditional theories is discussed. MCPT can provide a solid foundation for a wide range of methods and applications.

To validate this assertion, *Chapter 3* shows how the methodology of *data envelopment analysis* (DEA) can be generalised by MCPT. It facilitates to gain fruitful insights into some open questions of DEA as well as to avoid some pitfalls of its applications. Firstly, the relation between DEA and MCPT is explained, and it will be discussed what kind of data may be enveloped by a linear or convex hull. After that, the properties of well-known radial and additive DEA models and their systematic generalisations with respect to linear cost and benefit functions of increasing complexity are discussed.

Chapter 4 sketches selected further aspects and challenges that are essential for non-financial *performance evaluation in practice*:

- balance and specialisation as performance categories in addition to effectiveness and efficiency
- identification, selection and qualitative differentiation of the inputs and outputs that determine the considered costs and benefits
- influence of the choice of compared activities and of exogenous weighting factors on the relative performance
- approaches to detect dependencies of key performance indicators from the inputs and outputs, even though they are often not quantifiable
- and more comprehensive concepts of performance management and management accounting which may include the topics covered in this book.

References

Bamberg G, Coenenberg AG, Krapp M (2012) Betriebswirtschaftliche Entscheidungslehre. 15th ed, Vahlen, München

Datar SM, Rajan MV (2018) Horngren's Cost Accounting: A Managerial Emphasis. 16th ed, Pearson Prentice Hall, Essex, England

Dyckhoff H (1992) Betriebliche Produktion: Theoretische Grundlagen einer umweltorientierten Produktionswirtschaft. Springer, Berlin et al.

Dyckhoff H (2003) Eine moderne Konzeption der Produktionstheorie. In: Wildemann H (ed) Moderne Produktionskonzepte für Güter- und Dienstleistungsproduktionen. TCW-Verlag, München, pp 13–32

Dyckhoff H (2006) Produktionstheorie. 5th ed, Springer, Berlin et al.

Dyckhoff H, Ahn H (2002) Kosten-Nutzen-Analyse. In: Küpper HU, Wagenhofer A (ed) Handwörterbuch Unternehmensrechnung und Controlling. Schaeffer-Poeschel, Stuttgart, pp 113–122

Dyckhoff H, Ahn H (2010) Verallgemeinerte DEA-Modelle zur Performanceanalyse. Zeitschrift für Betriebswirtschaft 80:1249–1276

Dyckhoff H, Spengler T (2010) Produktionswirtschaft: Eine Einführung. 3rd ed, Springer, Berlin et al.

Dyckhoff H, Quandel A, Waletzke K (2015) Rationality of eco-efficiency methods: Is the BASF analysis dependent on irrelevant alternatives? International Journal of Life Cycle Assessment 20:1557–1567

Eisenführ F, Weber M, Langer T (2010) Rational Decision Making. Springer, Berlin et al.

EN ISO 14040 (2006) Environmental management – Life cycle assessment – Principles and framework. 2009-11

Ewert R, Wagenhofer A (2014) Interne Unternehmenrechnung. 8th ed, Springer, Berlin et al.

Hevner AR, March ST, Park J, Ram S (2004) Design science in information science research. MIS Quarterly 28:75–105

Kleine A (2004) A general framework for DEA. Omega 32:17–23

Neely A, Gregory M, Platts K (1995) Performance measurement system design: A literature review and research agenda. International Journal of Operations and Production Management 15:80–110

Riebel P (1994) Einzelkosten- und Deckungsbeitragsrechnung: Grundfragen einer markt- und entscheidungsorientierten Unternehmensrechnung. 7th ed, Gabler, Wiesbaden

Thies C, Kieckhäfer K, Spengler TS, Sodhi MS (2019): Operations research for sustainability assessment of products: A review. European Journal of Operational Research 274:1-21

Uhlman BW, Saling PR (2017) The BASF eco-efficiency toolbox: Holistic evaluation of sustainable solutions. In: Abraham M (ed): Encyclopedia of Sustainable Technologies, vol. 1. Elsevier, Amsterdam, pp 131–144

Weber M (1921; 4th ed 1980) Wirtschaft und Gesellschaft: Grundriss der verstehenden Soziologie. Mohr Siebeck, Tübingen

Weber M, Henderson AM, Parsons T (1964) The Theory of Social and Economic Organization. Collier-MacMillan, London (English translation of Weber 1921)

Chapter 2
Multi-criteria Production Theory: Foundation of Performance Evaluation[1]

Abstract. Multi-criteria production theory (MCPT) is a decision-theoretical generalisation of traditional production theories developed in order to integrate concerns of modern management science and economics, such as sustainability and environmental protection. Its main idea is to distinguish between the technologically determined inputs and outputs of a production system's activity and their desired or undesired impacts on artificial or natural environments. This is formalised by multiple value functions mapping the production possibility set (PPS) onto the value possibility set (VPS). Depending on the concretisation of the relevant objectives different kinds of economic, ecological or social concerns can be captured and analysed in view of the performance of the possible production activities as the decision alternatives at hand. Chapter 2 proves main theorems of MCPT and discusses the fundamentality of some axioms used in traditional production theories. The theorems are concerned with sufficient conditions for certain properties of the VPS, in particular its convexity or linearity. Furthermore, a monotonicity result for a hierarchy of valuations is derived. While an axiom of value disposability is plausible and helps to guarantee the convexity of the VPS, other axioms do not seem to be realistic or better must refer to the costs and benefits instead of the inputs and outputs.

Keywords Disposability • Efficiency • Production possibility set • Production theory • Value function

---

[1] This chapter is a revised version of essential parts from Dyckhoff (2018) by permission of the author. In addition, Sections 2.3.2 and 2.4.1 are adapted from Dyckhoff (2019) by permission of Springer Nature.

2.1   MCPT: A Particular Instance of General Production Theory

All production theories focus on ***processes of value creation by transforming objects*** (Dyckhoff 2003). The particular idea of multi-criteria production theory (MCPT) to generalise traditional production theories – such as, for example, the *Activity Analysis of Production and Allocation* of Koopmans (1951), the *Theory of Cost and Production Functions* of Shephard (1970) or the business-oriented production theory of Gutenberg (1951) – is to embed them consequently into the modern theory of decision making (Dyckhoff 1992). In this sense, MCPT is established by applying well-known theorems and methods of multi-criteria decision making (MCDM) and multi-attribute utility theory (MAUT) to decisions regarding production systems.

2.1.1   Conception and Fundamental Axioms

Dealing with *Industrial Production Models*, Dano (1966, p. 1) builds on a conception of production theory being largely compatible with modern management science and neighbouring disciplines:

> In microeconomics, the theory of production is often defined in a broad sense as identical with 'the theory of the firm'. Its purpose is to describe and explain entrepreneurial 'behaviour', usually in terms of an optimization model where some objective function (e.g. the profit function), which by hypothesis is the criterion of preference underlying the decisions of the firm, is maximized subject to the technological and market restrictions on the firm's behaviour.

While Koopmans (1951) and Shephard (1970) use 'production' as an undefined basic term, Frisch (1965, p. 3) characterises *(technical) production* in his *Theory of Production* as any transformation process that is desired by certain human beings and can be directed by them. He then proceeds:

> The term transformation indicates that there are certain things (goods or services) which enter into the process, and lose their identity in it, i.e. 'ceasing to exist' in their original form, while other things (goods or services) come into being in that they 'emerge' from the process. The first category may be referred to as 'production factors' (input elements), while the last-named category are referred to as 'products' (the output or resultant elements).

Hence, by definition, ***input*** enters into and ***output*** emerges out of the transformation process. Both the input of production factors and the output of products are usually understood as flows measured in time rates (Shephard 1970, p. 5). Besides (desired) ***goods and services***, the objects going into or coming out of the process may also be undesirable ***bads***. Their input and output flows are assessed opposite to those of goods. Thus, e.g., trim loss is an undesired output flow, but the input of waste to be incinerated is a desired flow because it decreases the stock of bads (Dyckhoff 1992, p. 67).

"By production in the *economic* sense", Frisch (1965, p. 8) means "the attempt to create a product which is *more highly valued* than the original input elements." This characterisation excludes consumption. In order to include recycling and disposal activities (such as waste incineration) – which do not necessarily generate desired products because of their main purpose to reduce or destroy bads (Souren 1996) – **production** *in general* is defined as value creation: That is any process directed and controlled by human beings which transforms (input into output) objects with the intention of generating advantages that outweigh the disadvantages of the transformation. Thus, higher positive values are created than consumed or more negative values are destroyed than newly induced as undesired by-products (Dyckhoff 1992, p. 7).

In this sense, illustrated by Figure 2.1, production theory in economics and management science studies *production systems*, i.e. systems consisting of *transformation processes* directed and controlled by *managers* in order to achieve certain predefined goals. These systems can be companies and their subsystems, such as plants or workplaces, but also whole (national or regional) economies.

Because restricted to a *particularly defined decision field* which is characterised by the specific technology of the considered transformation process, such a production system is a special case of a **decision-making unit** (DMU), studied generally

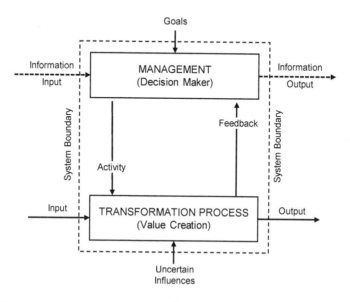

Fig. 2.1 Production system as decision-making unit (cf. Dyckhoff 1992, Fig. 19.1)

in decision theory. In this view, the principal approach to generalising traditional production theories, called *decision-based production theory*, is simply determined as an application of general decision theory to production systems as DMUs (cf. Sect. 1.2.1; see Dyckhoff 1992, p. 38, for its origin and early motivation).

Thus, production – and its performance – analysis is systematically embedded into decision theory, just as is already the case for most other subdisciplines of business economics and management science such as finance, marketing and management accounting (Dyckhoff 2003). This allows production theory not only to become compatible with the theories of these other subdisciplines but also to unlock all of the knowledge and know-how of both descriptive and prescriptive decision theory, including MCDM and MAUT. It provides a sound theoretical foundation for constructing operations management models as well as for analysing the rationality of production processes, in particular their effectiveness and efficiency. Production models, constructed in this way, are characterised as follows:

- Basically, they can be categorised into either descriptive and empirical models or prescriptive and normative ones. When designing such models, the general principles and methods of decision analysis may be helpful.
- The fundamental assumption of prescriptive decision theory is that a complex decision problem can be solved more effectively by decomposing it into five basic components (Eisenführ et al. 2010, p. 20): (1) the possible decision alternatives of the DMU, *here representing production activities*; (2) the potential uncertainties; (3) the consequences of the activities and the uncertainties; (4) the relevant objectives; and (5) the respective preferences of the decision maker or of an evaluator in the case of external performance evaluation (e.g. done by a stakeholder). Thus, production models can be structured along these five basic components. At least, they comprise a set of feasible production activities with associated preference relations.
- Such production models describe the transformation process and its corresponding activities only insofar as is necessary for the pending decision or (performance) evaluation to be made. In particular the decision-oriented view guides the model designer in defining and selecting the relevant inputs and outputs.

Positive values created as well as negative ones destroyed by the production system form the **benefits** of the transformation process. Conversely, **costs** are caused by consuming positive and generating negative values. Multiple benefits or costs defined in such a way do not need to be measured on one and the same scale. Instead they are often valued in their own distinct natural scales and thus are, *a priori*, not necessarily commensurable among each other[2] – unlike the special case of revenues and expenditures in monetary terms. Hence, with multiple incommensurable benefits and costs in decision-based production theory, the overall assessment of production activities always results in a multiple-criteria evaluation problem.

In concretisation of decision-based production theory, the basic instance of *multi-criteria production theory* (MCPT) is determined by the premise that all relevant data are assumed to be known, deterministic and measurable and that the benefits and costs depend on the actual inputs and outputs only (Dyckhoff 1992, p. 62; Dyckhoff and Ahn 2010). Thus, regarding the five basic components of production models in prescriptive decision theory (noted above), the following *fundamental assumptions* A1–A5 characterise this basic approach:

A1 (Production possibilities as decision alternatives): The set $\mathcal{P}$ of feasible production activities, called *production possibility set* (PPS), is completely described by m input and s output quantities $z = (x; y)$ of certain selected types of objects involved in the transformation process. Basically, $\mathcal{P}$ is part of a *technology* $\mathcal{T}$ which is defined by certain axioms (e.g. closeness or free disposal) and further individual characteristics (e.g. constant returns to scale) as predetermined general or specific properties:

$\mathcal{P} \subset \mathcal{T} = \{z = (x; y) \in \mathbb{R}_+^{m+s} \mid$ Input x can in principle be transformed into output $y\}$

$\mathcal{P}$ is often generated by some basic activities and restricted by constraints given for the decision at hand.

A2 (Deterministic, complete knowledge): There is no uncertainty in the data.

A3 (Relevant consequences depend on inputs and outputs only): The relevant consequences or results of any production activity considered by the decision maker or evaluator are completely captured by a multidimensional *value function* $v(z) \in \mathbb{R}^q$ of the respective input/output-vector $z = (x; y)$ that distinguishes all relevant results v caused by the inputs and outputs of the transformation process. The image $v(\mathcal{P})$ of the PPS is called *value possibility set* (VPS).

A4 (Costs/benefits-trade-off): The $q = k + \ell$ relevant consequences are differentiated into two distinct categories $v = (c; b)$, namely k types of (usually nonnegative) values destroyed, called *costs*, being disadvantageous results c, as

---

[2] This characterisation of costs and benefits is based on their definition in Section 1.1 and contrary to that of Shephard (1970), p. 10, who uses the term benefit "to indicate coverage of situations where the outputs do not have market prices but may have unit values (positive or negative) in accordance with some social weighting system, the negative values applying to undesirable outputs".

well as ℓ types of created values as (nonnegative) advantageous results $\boldsymbol{b}$, that are called **benefits**. Objectives are both the minimisation of each type of cost as well as the maximisation of each type of benefit.

A5 (Rational consistency): The preferences of the decision maker or evaluator are compatible with the vector dominance relations of the alternatives regarding the values, i.e. the costs/benefits-space.

Remark: The four-stage performance evaluation process, presented in Section 1.2.1 and characterised by the functional equations $(\boldsymbol{c}; \boldsymbol{b}) = \widetilde{v}(\boldsymbol{x}; \boldsymbol{y}) = v(r(\boldsymbol{x}; \boldsymbol{y}))$, is simplified in this and the following chapter. Assumption A3 does not explicitly address the results (or impacts) $r(\boldsymbol{x}; \boldsymbol{y})$ of an activity. Instead it is assumed that all relevant objective data of the decision context that are identical for all possible activities are integrated either into the value function (as done with $\widetilde{v} = v(r)$ in the last formula) or else into the input and output data themselves.

Besides the more structural assumptions A1–A5, no further general axioms have been stated for MCPT until now. Regularly, $\mathcal{P}$ and $\mathcal{T}$ should be **closed** and **non-trivial**, i.e. should contain at least two different production activities, and $v(\boldsymbol{z})$ should be **continuous** functions. Since the PPS $\mathcal{P}$ is defined as that part of the technology $\mathcal{T}$ which is realisable in the situation at hand, it is furthermore bounded in practice, e.g. by resource restrictions; then the VPS $v(\mathcal{P})$ is closed and **bounded**, too. Whether other axioms that are often used in traditional production theories should be applied in MCPT or even do make sense in reality, is questionable and will be discussed in Sections 2.4.1 and 3.2.3.

2.1.2 Illustrative Example of Sustainability Performance Evaluation

A realistic example with fictitious data shall demonstrate a case of (linear) value functions where certain inputs or outputs have conflicting impacts on different evaluation criteria.

Example 2.1: Sustainability performance of cement plants (Dyckhoff and Ahn 2010)

To be evaluated are cement plants referring to sustainability. Two types of benefits and costs each are decided to be relevant. The benefits include profit from the economic perspective (b_1), and job creation from the social perspective (b_2). From the ecological perspective, the two relevant types of costs are concerned with the contributions towards climate change (c_1) and to the ozone hole in the stratosphere above the Antarctic (c_2), respectively.

To quantify the corresponding consequences of the plants' production activities, the decision maker – or evaluator or model designer – considers as relevant three types of input, namely labour x_1, capital x_2 and scrap tyres x_3 as well as three types of output, cement y_1, carbon dioxide (CO_2) y_2 and chlorofluoro-carbon (CFC) y_3. The four value functions for each of the two types of benefits and costs depending on the six relevant types of inputs and outputs are calculated as follows:

$$b_1 = 340y_1 - 10x_1 - 50x_2 + 20x_3 \qquad c_1 = y_2 + 8500y_3$$
$$b_2 = x_1 \qquad\qquad\qquad\qquad\qquad c_2 = y_3 \qquad\qquad (2.1)$$

To determine the profit b_1, the combined total of worker salaries and capital costs are subtracted from the total revenues. The revenues not only result from sales of the cement output, but also from revenues acquired as fees for disposing of used scrap tyres that are incinerated as an input.[3] Job creation b_2 as second benefit can be judged from employment figures of labour input. The greenhouse effect c_1 is calculated from emissions of CO_2 and CFC, the latter having a negative pollution effect 8,500 times[4] higher than the former. Additionally, CFC causes a damage c_2 to the ozone layer.

Let us consider four cement plants. Figure 2.2 shows the matrices **X** and **Y** of their input and output quantities on the top, and on the bottom the two matrices **B** and **C** as their consequences for both types of benefit and cost, calculated by the four value functions of (2.1).

The example demonstrates three aspects which are unusual for traditional production theory: (1) Labour input x_1 has two opposing impacts: an undesired financial impact on profit b_1 and a desired social one on employment b_2. (2) The output CFC y_3 has two different, but both undesired ecological impacts simultaneously.

Production activities

$$\mathbf{X} = \begin{bmatrix} 4 & 4 & 5 & 3 \\ 3 & 5 & 5 & 5 \\ 5 & 1 & 3 & 3 \end{bmatrix} \begin{matrix} \text{Labour} \\ \text{Capital} \\ \text{Scrap tyres} \end{matrix}$$

$$\mathbf{Y} = \begin{bmatrix} 1 & 1 & 1 & 1 \\ 120 & 40 & 100 & 100 \\ 0.6 & 0.2 & 0.5 & 0.5 \end{bmatrix} \begin{matrix} \text{Cement} \\ CO_2 \\ \text{CFC} \end{matrix}$$

$\Downarrow$

Production consequences

$$\mathbf{B} = \begin{bmatrix} 250 & 70 & 100 & 120 \\ 4 & 4 & 5 & 3 \end{bmatrix} \begin{matrix} \text{Profit} \\ \text{Employment} \end{matrix}$$

$$\mathbf{C} = \begin{bmatrix} 4320 & 1140 & 3600 & 3600 \\ 0.6 & 0.2 & 0.5 & 0.5 \end{bmatrix} \begin{matrix} \text{Climate effect} \\ \text{Ozone effect} \end{matrix}$$

Fig. 2.2 Four cement plants as decision-making units (cf. Dyckhoff 2018, Fig. 3)

---

[3] Though the scrap tyres serve as fuel for the process of cement production, this does not change their character as a bad.

[4] The value 8,500 is a roughly rounded average of the six values of different CFCs that are presented in the fifth assessment report of the Intergovernmental Panel on Climate Change (Myrhe et al. 2013, p. 731).

(3) Scrap tyres are considered here as an undesired factor whose input x_3 into incineration is thus desired in order to destroy them and hence to add value by reducing negative values.

Remark: Employment is interpreted as an outcome, not as an output of the input labour. Here, the term 'outcome' of an activity is synonymously used to describe the impacts for the adjacent environments of a production system and is distinguished from the term 'output'. Otherwise, the reduction of the stock of scrap tyres via their incineration would also have to be called output (and not outcome only), which would be counterintuitive. In this sense, damages to nature caused by economic activities are outcomes but not outputs (for instance, in environmental science an *emission* such as sulphur dioxide at the 'end-of-pipe' of a production process is distinguished from its *immission* in the atmosphere, which causes acid rain).

2.1.3   Value Dominance and Value Efficiency

A central topic of production theory is the efficiency of possible activities. For example, which of the four cement plants of Figure 2.2 is efficient in comparison to the other three? For that purpose, one has to answer the fundamental question of how efficiency is defined in MCPT. In view of the decision-based approach, it is obvious to make use of the standard notion from decision theory (Dyckhoff 1992, p. 89):

Definition: A production activity is *(strongly) value efficient* with respect to $\mathcal{P}$ and the multi-dimensional costs and benefits as relevant objectives when (i.e. if and only if) there is no other alternative in $\mathcal{P}$ dominating it. Thereby, alternative a *value-dominates* alternative b *(weakly)* when alternative a is better than b for at least one of the objectives and not worse regarding all others.

Thus, an activity $(x; y)$ of a PPS is referred to as value efficient (or "functionally efficient"; Fandel 2010, p. 89) if, and only if, its image $v(x; y)$ is efficient with respect to the corresponding VPS in the space of relevant objectives. In traditional production theory more specific notions such as, for example, input-efficiency or proper efficiency are also defined (Esser 2001, p. 119). In particular, the following one is of essential importance in connection with radial efficiency measures (cf. Chap. 3):

Definition: An activity is called *weakly value efficient* when it is not strongly value-dominated (regarding all relevant objectives and all other possible activities). Thereby, an activity *value-dominates* another one *strongly* when it is truly better for each of the relevant objectives.

Therefore, one also speaks of strong efficiency and weak dominance regarding the standard notion above. As can be seen, other notions of traditional theory are easily be generalised for MCPT if they are defined with respect to the VPS instead of the PPS. Then, the benefits and the costs of the production activities are compared, and not their outputs and inputs: Input/output-efficiency becomes *cost/benefit-efficiency*. If all objectives which comprise the relevant ends, means, and secondary results of an activity have been taken into account, value efficiency represents a mathematical formalisation of Max Weber's concept of purposive rationality, introduced in Section 1.1; in particular, one obtains:

Definition: An activity is called ***effective*** when it is value efficient regarding the ends as sole values (hence excluding means and secondary results).

2.2 Linear Value Functions and Their Special Cases

In all well-known theories of production and cost, properties A1–A5 are fulfilled, too, but are concretised by additional, very particular assumptions concerning the value function as well as the PPS. However, a lot of more special cases of MCPT can be derived by varying those assumptions, namely regarding different specifications of the multi-dimensional value function $v(x; y)$ on the one hand or the fundamental axioms and the particular properties specifying the technology $\mathcal{T}$ and the PPS $\mathcal{P}$ on the other hand.

2.2.1 Traditional and Environmental Production Theories

With respect to the value function, no more than the following two extreme cases of a continuum of other possible special cases are traditionally considered (Dyckhoff and Spengler 2010, pp. 83 and 105).[5] At the one extreme, called *success theory* (Dyckhoff 1992, p. 115), there exists only one single one-dimensional value function to be maximised, measuring the **success** as overall benefit generated by the inputs and outputs of the production process, usually determined by the profit or contribution margin (i.e. assumption A4 reduces to the trivial case: $q = \ell = 1$, $k = 0$). If the revenues are supposed to be fixed, one obtains the *traditional cost theories* ($q = k = 1$, $\ell = 0$).

---

[5] Only a few exceptions are analysed until now (Dyckhoff 2018). Hasenkamp (1992) considers the special case of MCPT with two (economic) benefit and no cost functions. Another such example is the *Success and environmentally oriented production theory* of Dinkelbach and Rosenberg (2004), where profit as economic benefit and pollution as ecological cost form two objectives (cf. Fandel 2010, p. 83, for a short review of distinct environmental production theories).

At the other extreme, the ***traditional production theories*** consider the alternative simplest case of what may constitute the relevant consequences of a production activity:

A6a (Trade-off of goods only): Each selected type of objects uniquely forms one of the $k = m$ types of costs on the input side, i.e. $c = x$, or one of the $\ell = s$ types of benefits on the output side, i.e. $b = y$.

Here, costs and benefits are caused by the consumption (= input) and production (= output) of goods within the transformation process (*goods* being positively valued objects, items, things, entities). Hence, the essential distinction between the approaches to MCPT characterised by A1–A5 and that to the traditional theories lies in the fact that multiple, in general incommensurable costs $c(z)$ and benefits $b(z)$ are to be minimised or maximised instead of the original inputs and outputs $z = (x; y)$ themselves, the latter two merely describing the production activity by their direct consequences. In this particular case of traditional production theory, where the inputs and outputs themselves are regarded as sole measures for costs and benefits, i.e. $c(x; y) = x$ and $b(x; y) = y$, value efficiency reduces to the usual efficiency notion of Koopmans (1951). To differentiate this notion from those with more information on the values created or consumed by the production activity – such as 'allocative efficiency' when prices are known – the term *technical efficiency* is sometimes used for differentiation in the literature (Fandel and Lorth 2009).

This basic kind of valuation in traditional production theory does, however, not fit properly for ecological evaluations. Here, the indirect consequences of inputs and outputs, called *environmental* pressures or *impacts*, are actually of importance, namely the outcomes for nature of resource depletion or emissions into the atmosphere (Kuosmanen and Kortelainen 2005). Instead of using these impacts as original values (in line with assumptions A3 and A4), environmental performance evaluations often take only the quantities of inputs and outputs themselves as proxies, but differentiate $z = (z^G; z^B)$ into those of goods $z^G = (x^G; y^G)$ and those of bads $z^B = (x^B; y^B)$. The corresponding standard assumption[6] for such an ***environmental production theory*** then becomes:

A6b (Trade-off of goods and bads): Each input of a good and each output of a bad uniquely defines one corresponding type of the costs, i.e. $c = (x^G; y^B)$, and, vice versa, each output of a good as well as each input of a bad one type of the benefits, i.e. $b = (x^B; y^G)$.

---

[6] Dyckhoff (1992, p. 65) has called it *standard assumption* ("Normalfall"; Esser 2001, p. 97) because of its ubiquity in the respective environmentally oriented literature, but not because of its representativeness for reality (p. 69). He has pointed to the prominent example of the so-called flue-gas desulphurisation (FDG) gypsum as a by-product of coal-fired power plants (p. 6), whose desirability depends on the actual market conditions (Fandel and Lorth 2009, p. 416).

All the particular notions of (technical, allocative etc.) efficiency can be generalised for assumption A6b in cases of environmental production theories such that the dominance direction of bads for an input or an output is contrary to that of goods. Thus, analogously to traditional theory, in cases of bads, efficient productions can also be termed as technically efficient. Furthermore, other special notions, e.g. *environmental efficiency* or *pollutant efficiency*, may also be differentiated.[7] These environmental production theories, as special cases of MCPT, will be subject of further studies in Section 3.3 as well as in parts of Chapter 4.

2.2.2 Main Proposition for Linear Value Functions

In this and the following sections we will analyse the implications of more general specifications concerning assumptions (A6) regarding the properties of the multi-dimensional value function.

A6c (Linear values): $v(\lambda_1 z_1 + \lambda_2 z_2) = \lambda_1 v(z_1) + \lambda_2 v(z_2)$ for all $z_j \in \mathcal{P}$, $\lambda_j \geq 0$, $j \in \{1,2\}$.

Assumption A6c characterises **linear** value functions: $v(z) = V \cdot z$, where V is a **value impact matrix**.

Until now, no assumption specifies the technology and the PPS in any way, except for non-triviality, closeness and eventually boundedness (mentioned at the end of Sect. 2.1.1). The following two further assumptions (A7) are of material importance, as their ubiquity in the relevant literature seems to attest.

A7a (Convex production): The production possibility set $\mathcal{P}$ is convex.

In connection with linear values, this importance is emphasised by our first main proposition.

Theorem 2.1: Assume A6c and A7a, i.e. let $v(z)$ be multiple linear value functions defined on a convex PPS $\mathcal{P}$ (in input/output-space). Then, the VPS $\mathcal{V} = v(\mathcal{P})$ is a convex set (in value space), too.

Proof: Let $v_i \in \mathcal{V}$, $i \in \{1,2\}$, be two arbitrary achievable value points and $v_3 = \alpha v_1 + (1 - \alpha)v_2$ for $0 \leq \alpha \leq 1$ any of their convex combinations in value space. Then, there exist two corresponding possible production activities $z_i \in \mathcal{P}$ with $v(z_i) = v_i$. Thus, with $z_3 := \alpha z_1 + (1 - \alpha)z_2 \in \mathcal{P}$ because of A7a, from A6c follows: $v_3 = \alpha v_1 + (1 - \alpha)v_2 = \alpha v(z_1) + (1 - \alpha)v(z_2) = v(\alpha z_1 + (1 - \alpha)z_2) = v(z_3)$. Hence $v_3 \in \mathcal{V}$, too.

---

[7] Cf. Dyckhoff (1992), p. 91; Dinkelbach and Rosenberg (2004), p. 56. Esser (2001) elaborates the decision-based production theory of Dyckhoff (1992) by considering various kinds of preference relations for the consequences of the production. Thereby, he develops a mathematically founded systematisation of different notions of efficiency as well as of various environmentally oriented production theories in the German literature.

Remark: As the proof of the theorem indicates, it is analogously true for a linear instead of a convex PPS, then implying a linear VPS.

To simplify the presentation, a fairly general type of business technologies $\mathcal{T}$ with convex PPS $\mathcal{P}$ can often be taken as a basis. Here, $\mathcal{P}$ is generated (or spanned) by a finite number $j = 1,\dots,n$ of basic activities $\mathbf{z}_j = (\mathbf{x}_j; \mathbf{y}_j) \in \mathbb{R}^{m+s}$ (Fandel 2010, p. 49; Dyckhoff and Spengler 2010, p. 162), i.e. it is determined as a certain **_envelopment_** of these activities that can be mathematically described as follows:

$$\mathcal{P} = \left\{ \mathbf{z} = \sum_{j=1}^{n} \lambda_j \mathbf{z}_j \,\middle|\, \lambda \in S \right\} \quad \text{for} \quad S := \left\{ \lambda \in \mathbb{R}_+^n \,\middle|\, \tau_{min} \le \sum_{j=1}^{n} \lambda_j \le \tau_{max} \right\} \tag{2.2}$$

S defines the set of admissible *activity levels* $\lambda = (\lambda_1, \dots, \lambda_n)$. Four cases are of particular interest which are determined by combining the two lower bounds $\tau_{min} \in \{0; 1\}$ with the two upper bounds $\tau_{max} \in \{1; \infty\}$. Each of the four different ranges for the activity levels λ_j implies a PPS $\mathcal{P}$ with either *variable* (VRS: 1;1), *non-increasing* (NIRS: 0;1), *non-decreasing* (NDRS: 1;∞), or else *constant* (CRS: 0;∞) **_returns to scale_**. $\mathcal{P}$ is linear in the last and convex in all four cases. Thus, the next assumption is a special case of A7a.

A7b (Finitely generated convex PPS): The PPS $\mathcal{P}$ is spanned by a finite number of non-trivial basic activities following (2.2) for one of the four principal cases of variable, non-increasing, non-decreasing or constant returns to scale.

The cases CRS and VRS with $S = \mathbb{R}_+^n$ or $S = \left\{ \lambda \in \mathbb{R}_+^n \,\middle|\, \sum_{j=1}^n \lambda_j = 1 \right\}$ play eminent roles in the data envelopment methodology of performance measurement, which Chapter 3 deals with.

2.3   Nonlinear Value Functions and Their Special Cases

Theorem 2.1 has shown that, with linear value functions, the VPS inherits essential properties of the underlying PPS. This substantially simplifies the performance analysis. Therefore, and because of their importance for applications in practice, we mostly use linear value functions in the following chapters. Nevertheless, as they cannot always be applied in reality, we next emphasise the problems concerning nonlinear valuations and prove some theorems for convex and monotonic cases.

2.3.1 Difficulties in Cases of Nonlinear Value Functions

The simple graphical *example* of Figure 2.3 already illustrates that the properties of
the *PPS* (below-left quadrant) may differ substantially from those of the *VPS*
(above-right quadrant) as its image.

Example 2.2: Deriving a nonconvex VPS from a convex PPS

Figure 2.3 illustrates three activities A, B, and C of decision-making units
(DMUs), each of which produces one kind of product in quantity y from one
kind of factor in quantity x, displayed below-left in the two-dimensional coordinate system. As numerical instance let input and output $z = (x; y)$ of the
three DMUs be given by $z_A = (4; 2)$, $z_B = (12; 3)$, and $z_C = (18; 9)$. According to property A7b, the PPS $\mathcal{P}$ is determined as the *triangle* generated by
the convex envelopment of the three activities for a technology with variable
returns to scale (below-left in Fig. 2.3).

The production causes a cost c, which is proportional to the input x; for reasons of simplicity let the *cost function* be $c(x; y) = x$ (below-right in Fig. 2.3).
A quadratic *benefit function* $b(x; y) = y(10 - y)$ determines the dependence
of a benefit b from the output y (above-left in Fig. 2.3). Then, points $\tilde{A}$, $\tilde{B}$,
and $\tilde{C}$ in *value space* (above-right in Fig. 2.3) build the images of the production activities A, B, and C. All other points of the PPS (below-left triangle) are
mapped onto corresponding points in the above-right quadrant, too. In this way,
one obtains the VPS with a (shaded) nonconvex shape, representing the value
image of the PPS.[8] Only those combinations which are on the bold part of the
above-left curve of the nonconvex shape are efficient with respect to benefit and
cost. This bold curve in the above-right quadrant represents the value image of
the bold strict subsegment of the *line between A and C* in the below-left triangle.
Hence, although the whole line segment between A and C (with $y = 0.5x$ for
$4 \le x \le 18$) is traditionally regarded as 'technically efficient' (with respect to
an input to be minimised and an output to be maximised), only its bold subsegment spanning from A up to the point of maximal benefit (i.e. points D and $\tilde{D}$
in Figure 2.3 with $z_D = (10; 5)$) really is value efficient (regarding benefit and
cost).

---

[8] It should be noted that the representation of the VPS is two-dimensional (namely one type of
benefit and cost each). The indicated three-dimensional effect in the above-right quadrant of Figure
2.3 was merely chosen to better illustrate the derivation of the VPS from the PPS.

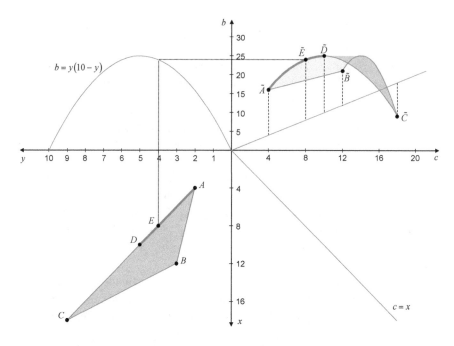

Fig. 2.3 Example with nonlinear value function (cf. Dyckhoff 2018, Fig. 5)

Let us consider three different interpretations of Figure 2.3.

Example 2.3 (2.2 continued): Traditional profit maximisation of monopolists[9]
The graphs of Figure 2.3 can be interpreted in classical economic terms, namely in the sense of the well-known Cournot Theorem for price fixing by a monopolistic market actor. Here, the three DMUs A, B and C may represent distinct business units selling quantities y of the product on their own local markets, determined by a linear demand function ($y = 10 - p$, with $p = $ product price per unit) with respect to the individual price set by each business unit on its market. The vertical, upwards-directed axis shows the *revenue* $b(y)$, and the horizontal, right-directed axis the *financial costs* $c(x)$ of the input x. If the measurement of benefits and costs use the same (monetary) scale, the difference $b - c$ determines the *profit* or *contribution margin*. In the above-right quadrant of Figure 2.3, this is shown for each of the three DMUs as vertical segments to the angle bisector, marked with dashed lines, for DMU C to indicate a loss, for the other two – and also for the benefit-maximum (i.e. revenue-maximum) D – to indicate a positive margin. The dotted lines in the coordinate system indicate the so-called Cournot point E as the point of maximal profit (derived from $\tilde{E}$ in Figure 2.3)

---

[9] Cf. Dyckhoff (1992), p. 62, for a similar example, but with two inputs and a pollutant as joint (by-)product.

regarding the below-left triangle as PPS: $z_E = (8; 4)$ with $c = 8$, $b = 24$ and $(b - c)^{max} = 16$.

In contrast, such a one-dimensional optimisation is not possible in the following two interpretations of Figure 2.3, because there exists no (simple) aggregation of benefit and cost.

Example 2.4 (2.2 and 2.3 continued): Eco-efficient frontier

Still suppose that the DMUs are receiving revenues b from selling a product in quantity y by fixing a certain price. Now production takes place with fixed financial costs by exploiting a natural resource as free good in quantity x. However, the exploitation of the natural resource induces ecological costs c that cannot be measured in monetary terms. Then, the determination of one single optimal activity is no longer possible – at least not in such an easy way as with Example 2.3. Instead, there are many value efficient activities on the *curve between $\tilde{A}$ and $\tilde{D}$* (above-right in Fig. 2.3). Calculating this efficient frontier in value space leads to the concave function $b = 0.5c(10 - 0.5c)$ with $4 \leq c \leq 10$. It quantifies the trade-off between economic revenue b and ecological damage c, being of diminishing rate $b' = 5 - 0.5c$.

Example 2.5 (2.2 – 2.4 continued): Research performance evaluation[10]

Figure 2.3 may also be considered from the view of non-financial performance analysis without any monetary valuation. In such an alternative interpretation, we might imagine that the three DMUs represent researchers who, over the course of a year, have produced a quantity y of academic papers by investing an amount of time x. According to these input and output quantities, researcher B has been less productive than the other two. But since the academic content of a collection of papers is certainly not proportional to their number, one should preferably choose other performance criteria, e.g. the *academic knowledge content b* of the papers as a benefit, and the *effort c* invested by the researcher while writing the papers as a cost or disutility. These two non-financial criteria are shown in the extended coordinate system of Figure 2.3 with axes in the north and east directions (up and right). For simplicity, it is supposed that the effort c of a researcher is equal to the time x invested (below-right). It is furthermore assumed that the total scientific innovation content b of a researcher's papers depends only on their number per year y, increasing with a diminishing rate at first as the number increases, but then decreasing absolutely past a certain maximum threshold until some maximal number of yearly written papers which collectively contain no new knowledge ($y_{max} = 10$ papers in Fig. 2.3). The easiest

---

[10] It should be noted that the example is purely didactic in nature and not intended to make any sort of commentary about real life!

way to describe this is with a quadratic value function (above-left). Then, the VPS contains all achievable combinations of knowledge contribution b and effort c invested. Comparing only the three researchers, A and B can be identified as (value) efficient, while C works inefficiently. If it seems allowable to 'construct' virtual researchers by the convex combinations of the invested time and produced papers of the three observed researchers, B becomes (value) inefficient, too. In this case, only those researchers are efficient whose time/paper-combination leads to a point on the bold subsegment spanning from A to D; a further performance distinction between them is not possible without comparing the trade-off between benefit and cost.

Two questions arise due to the example in Figure 2.3: (1) Are there types of nonlinear value functions, which guarantee that a linear or convex PPS is mapped onto a VPS which is linear or convex, too? (2) What kind of nonlinear value functions is sufficient for a proposition that states a general relation between the value efficiency of an activity and its 'technical efficiency'? Answers to both questions are given in the next two subsections.

2.3.2 Main Propositions for Convex Value Possibilities

Already a single quadratic value function in the example of Figure 2.3 implies that the VPS is not convex although the underlying PPS itself is convex. For example, all convex combinations of the two image points $\tilde{A}$ and $\tilde{C}$ in value space cannot be realised by a feasible production activity, although the convex combinations of their origins A and C are not only possible but, moreover, technically efficient. As one can see in the value space (above-right), it is not only the efficient points that are outside of the triangle built by the images $\tilde{A}$, $\tilde{B}$, and $\tilde{C}$ of the three observed production alternatives but also all other points of the VPS. Nevertheless, the *efficient frontier* of the VPS – consisting of all efficient points of $v(\mathcal{P})$ – is concave. Since the quadratic benefit function is concave and the cost function linear, this is no coincidence, but an implication of the next property.

A6d (Convexity of values): The individual benefit functions $b(x; y)$ are concave and the individual cost functions $c(x; y)$ are convex; i.e. with $w(z) := \left(-c(z); b(z)\right)$, for any $0 \le \alpha \le 1$ and $z_i \in \mathcal{P}$, $i \in \{1, 2\}$, the following holds: $w(\alpha z_1 + (1 - \alpha)z_2) \ge \alpha w(z_1) + (1 - \alpha)w(z_2)$.

Theorem 2.2: Assume A6d and A7a, i.e. let $c(z)$ and $b(z)$ be multiple convex cost and concave benefit functions defined on a convex PPS $\mathcal{P}$. Then, the efficient frontier of the corresponding VPS $v(\mathcal{P})$ is convex regarding the costs and concave regarding the benefits, too.

Proof: Let $v_i = (c_i; b_i)$ for $i \in \{1, 2, 3\}$ be any three points on the efficient frontier of $v(\mathcal{P})$. There exist corresponding activities $z_i \in \mathcal{P}$ with $c_i = c(z_i)$ and $b_i = b(z_i)$. If $z_3 = \alpha z_1 + (1 - \alpha)z_2$ for any $0 \leq \alpha \leq 1$, properties A6d and A7a imply: $w(z_3) \geq \alpha w(z_1) + (1 - \alpha)w(z_2)$ for $w(z) = (-c(z); b(z))$. Thus, points on the efficient frontier cannot be dominated by convex combinations of two other efficient points.

From the nonconvex VPS of Figure 2.3 we know that the convex combination of realisable cost/benefit-vectors does not need to be realisable itself. This is avoided if the following property can be assumed for an extended VPS $\widehat{v(\mathcal{P})}$:

A8 (Value disposability): All benefits attainable by production can be reduced and all costs induced by production can be augmented, i.e. all value points of the following enlarged VPS, dominated by the original VPS, are realisable, too:

$$\widehat{v(\mathcal{P})} = \left\{ (c; b) \in \mathbb{R}_+^{k+\ell} \mid c \geq c(x; y), b \leq b(x; y), (x; y) \in \mathcal{P} \right\}$$

Figure 2.4 shows the amendment of the VPS of Figure 2.3 by an additional value disposability assumption, i.e. the *shaded area right and below the VPS*. The PPS itself does not have changed.

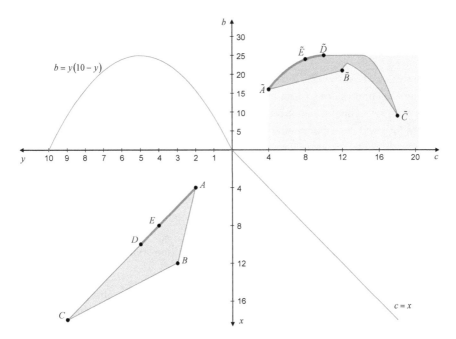

Fig. 2.4 Example with disposable nonlinear values (cf. Dyckhoff 2019, Fig. 2)

Theorem 2.3: Assume A6d and A7a as well as A8, i.e. let $c(z)$ and $b(z)$ be multiple convex cost and concave benefit functions defined on a convex PPS $\mathcal{P}$ (in input/output-space). Then, the extension $\widehat{v(\mathcal{P})}$ of the VPS $v(\mathcal{P})$ by the disposability of benefits and costs is a convex set (in value space), too.

Proof: Let $v_i = (c_i; b_i) \in \widehat{v(\mathcal{P})}$, $i \in \{1, 2\}$, be two arbitrary achievable value points and $v_3 = \alpha v_1 + (1 - \alpha)v_2$ for $0 \le \alpha \le 1$ any of their convex combinations in value space. Then, there exist two corresponding production activities $z_i \in \mathcal{P}$, $i \in \{1, 2\}$, dominating these two arbitrary value points such that $b(z_i) \ge b_i$ and $c(z_i) \le c_i$, i.e. $w(z_i) \ge w_i := (-c_i; b_i)$. With $z_3 := \alpha z_1 + (1 - \alpha)z_2$, from A6d follows: $w_3 = \alpha w_1 + (1 - \alpha)w_2 \le \alpha w(z_1) + (1 - \alpha)w(z_2) \le w(\alpha z_1 + (1 - \alpha)z_2) = w(z_3)$. Thus, since $z_3 \in \mathcal{P}$, v_3 is dominated by $v(z_3) \in v(\mathcal{P})$. Hence, $v_3 \in \widehat{v(\mathcal{P})}$. ∎

Value disposability presupposes that there exist certain additional activities, which are realisable by the considered DMUs although they are not explicitly modelled. Therefore, they are no original elements of the PPS, i.e. not represented by the production technology and the actual restrictions. Instead they are elements of that part of the production environment which a DMU can yet influence. In Example 2.3 (and also in Example 2.4), this may be the possibility of a monopolist to give away the money received as revenue for the product without further reward. In Example 2.4, the augmentation of ecological cost can result from a larger damage when exploiting nature or by extracting more of the resource than is used as input by the DMU.

2.3.3 Main Propositions for Consistent Monotonic Valuations

Example 2.1 of Section 2.1.2 illustrates an instance of two conflicting interests regarding the input labour of the cement plants. The profit $b_1 = 340y_1 - 10x_1 - 50x_2 + 20x_3$ as one of two types of benefits increases with the output quantity of cement (y_1) and the input quantity of scrap tyres (x_3) and decreases with the input quantities of both labour and capital (x_1, x_2). In contrast, the benefit employment (b_2) increases with more labour input (x_1). This characterises the diverging interests of shareholders and workers and hence an inconsistent valuation of the input labour, which is why the example of four cement plants in Figure 2.2 exhibits no direct dominance relations between the inputs and outputs themselves (but perhaps *win-win* possibilities between profit and employment).

The following property of linear as well as of nonlinear value functions excludes such a preference inconsistency.

A6e (Consistent valuation): There is no input and no output that simultaneously contributes to several types of costs and benefits with a conflict of interests.

In these instances, the fundamental assumption A4 of Section 2.1.1 for cost minimisation and benefit maximisation implies a corresponding unique preference for minimising or alternatively maximising each single input and output. In the special cases of A6a and A6b, property A6e is always fulfilled.

Because of the constant coefficients of the value impact matrix V of linear value functions (A6c), the consequence of increasing an input or an output is always of the same sign regarding a particular type of value. This property is satisfied in general for all monotonic (although perhaps nonlinear) value functions.

A6f (Strictly monotonic values): For each type of cost or benefit, value function $v(x; y)$ is either strictly decreasing or strictly increasing or constant with respect to changes of any single input or output.

In Example 2.3, the profit maximum of the monopolistic firm is value efficient (regarding revenues and costs as two separate objectives) as well as technically efficient (regarding input and output). It is an important question as to whether there are certain general relationships between the efficiencies of different valuation levels. Indeed, if the costs and benefits of a higher valuation level depend monotonically in a consistent manner on the costs and benefits of the lower levels, the following proposition states that every production activity that dominates another one on a lower level also dominates on levels above. Thereby **consistent** means that higher costs of a lower level lead to higher costs or lower benefits on upper levels – and analogously for higher benefits.

Theorem 2.4: For any PPS $\mathcal{P}$, let $v^1(x; y)$ and $v^2(x; y)$ with $v^2(x; y) = u(v^1(x; y))$ be two multiple value functions, where $u(v)$ is a strictly monotonic, separable function mapping the first level costs and benefits determined by $v^1(x; y)$ consistently onto the second level costs and benefits determined by $v^2(x; y)$. Then, if activity $(x_A; y_A) \in \mathcal{P}$ of DMU A dominates activity $(x_B; y_B) \in \mathcal{P}$ of DMU B with respect to the first value level, A dominates B with respect to the second value level, too.

Proof: Let $c^i(z)$ and $b^i(z)$ for $i \in \{1, 2\}$ be the 1st and 2nd level costs and benefits of activities $z \in \mathcal{P}$ such that $v^i = (c^i; b^i)$ and $v^2 = u(v^1)$. Dominance of A over B regarding the first value level is equivalent to the following vector dominance of (negatively valued) costs and (positively valued) benefits: $(-c_A^1; b_A^1) \geq (-c_B^1; b_B^1)$. Consistent monotonicity and separability of $u(v)$ imply that any type of 2nd level cost is strictly increasing regarding those of 1st level costs and strictly decreasing regarding those of 1st level benefits on which it depends; and vice versa for the 2nd level benefits. From this follows the asserted 2nd level value dominance of A over B, namely: $c_A^2 = u^c(c_A^1; b_A^1) \leq u^c(c_B^1; b_B^1) = c_B^2$ and $b_A^2 = u^b(c_A^1; b_A^1) \geq u^b(c_B^1; b_B^1) = b_B^2$.

Thus, monotonicity and (nonlinear) separability form a kind of conditions for *preferential consistency* which are sufficient for the fact that dominance relations are transferred from one valuation level to the next. It has immediate implications for the respective efficiencies of both value levels (cf. Sect. 3.4).

Corollary 2.5: Let there be two preferentially consistent first- and second-level multiple value functions, as defined in Theorem 2.4.

(a) If a production activity is efficient regarding (the PPS and) the second valuation level, then it is also efficient regarding the first one.

(b) In the special cases of traditional and environmental production theory with first level value functions satisfying assumption A6a or A6b, each production activity being value efficient with respect to the second valuation level is technically efficient, too.

In particular, if the second level determines the success (e.g. profit of the DMUs) by a one-dimensional value function, then the success maximum is always technically efficient.[11]

Corollary 2.6: An inefficient production activity remains inefficient if its inputs and outputs, or its values on a higher level, are further aggregated by preferentially consistent monotonic value functions.

2.4　First Insights and Conclusions

The propositions derived in the last sections allow for some first conclusions which will be extended in the next chapters.

2.4.1　Empirical Realism of Purely Technological Axioms

'Input without Output' as well as 'No Output without Input' are usual axioms of traditional production theory (see e.g. Färe and Grosskopf 1996, p. 12). They would contradict the mass and energy balance principles of physics if all material objects of the production process were to be relevant for the question at hand (Baumgärtner et al. 2001). Otherwise, if one is solely interested in, for example, the additional fuel needed for a waste incineration plant necessary to reach high enough temperatures, only the two inputs of fuel and waste might be relevant, but none of the outputs (such as heat or carbon dioxide). Probably, the motivation for both above axioms is more of an economic rather than a technological nature. This becomes especially apparent for the second one because it was originally referred to as the 'Impossibility of the Land of Cockaigne' by Koopmans (1951). Instead of 'No Output without

---

[11] Dyckhoff (1992, p. 121) has called the last relationship *compatibility between the weak and the strong rationality principle*, which, in the case of traditional economic theory, equals the compatibility between the principles of technical efficiency and profit-maximising behaviour.

Input' one would better postulate *No Benefit without Cost* (Dyckhoff 1992, p. 75). This would allow for a PPS solely with inputs, namely the inputs both of goods *and* bads, e.g. of fuel and waste, resulting both in benefits from the reduction of bads as well as in costs from the consumption of goods. Analogously, the axiom 'Input without Output' could be generalised to *Cost without Benefit*.

Analyses in production economics, especially those of neoclassical theory, often make use of further technological axioms, in particular regarding the disposability of inputs and outputs (e.g. Färe and Grosskopf 1996, p. 13). Indeed, the unwanted and ecologically harmful output of technologically unavoidable by-products can be ignored in economics if it can be disposed of without costs; then, however, it is not to be considered 'bad' but *neutral* in an economic evaluation (Dyckhoff and Allen 2001, p. 315). Although such a *free* (or *strong*) *disposability* does also make sense with respect to (immaterial) services as inputs or outputs of a transformation process, it is nowadays often no longer the case for material objects, namely in view of resource scarcity and environmental protection. This is a main reason why various other disposability assumptions (reviewed by Dakpo et al. 2016) have been developed for environmental performance analysis. In particular, Shephard's (1970, p. 187) *weak disposability* assumption is commonly used, despite that it is largely questioned with regard to its ability to account for detrimental outputs (Dakpo et al. 2016, p. 356).

Reality shows that disposability assumptions for the PPS cannot be generic but should be carefully justified by technological arguments relating to the physical production process in question. To this end, the model designer needs to have a deep understanding of all affected spheres of reality. An example illustrates this argument.

Example 2.6: Output disposability of coal power plants

Due to global warming, CO_2 is an undesirable output of the process of generating electricity by burning coal. For reasons rooted in the fundamental physics and chemistry of the process, it is an (unavoidable) by-product of power in the oxidation of coal. However, by adding 'carbon capture and storage' (CCS) as an abatement transformation process, carbon dioxide can be prevented from entering the atmosphere and, hence, from contributing to the greenhouse effect. Instead, the carbon dioxide is captured and pumped into underground caverns, such as old salt domes or oil fields. This does not affect the actual process of electricity generation but adds an extra 'end-of-pipe technology' to the production chain. In this way, the CO_2 otherwise emitted into the atmosphere can be reduced to one tenth of its previous quantity. However, the process of CCS itself requires large amounts of energy, reducing the net amount of electricity generated. The energy efficiency of modern coal-burning plants that implement this technique decreases by about 10 percentage points, from around 45 % to 35 %.[12] CCS is thus an example of a *technology-specific type of disposability* where the desirable output is scaled back by roughly a quarter in order to reduce the undesirable output by around 90 % (but still not completely eliminating it). If a set of such power plants as DMUs is to be evaluated by methods of non-financial performance evaluation, e.g. DEA, there is no necessity to (explicitly) assume an additional kind of disposability for the PPS, because all possible disposal activities (by CCS) should already be (implicitly) contained in the envelopment of the observed DMUs' activities.

Actually of importance in ecological evaluations are the environmental pressures or impacts as production outcomes for nature – of resource depletion on the input side and of emissions into soil, water, and the atmosphere on the output side. Anyhow, instead of using these impacts as original values, environmental performance assessments usually take the quantities of inputs and outputs themselves as proxies, thereby differentiating $z = (z^G; z^B)$ into those of goods $z^G = (x^G; y^G)$ and those of bads $z^B = (x^B; y^B)$. An implicit assumption of such *production theories with goods and bads* then reads as follows: Each input of a good and each output of a bad uniquely defines one corresponding type of the costs, i.e. $c = (x^G; y^B)$, and, vice versa, each output of a good as well as each input of a bad one type of the benefits, i.e. $b = (x^B; y^G)$. In this special case A6b of MCPT (cf. Sect. 2.2.1), the assumption A8 of *Disposability of Benefits and Costs* in Section 2.3.2 equals the assumption of **Extended Strong Disposability**, which itself is a straightforward generalisation of the well-known *strong or free disposability* axiom (Liu et al. 2010). Thus, property A8, here newly introduced for the value space, only requires the disposability of impacts outside of the considered production system and may thus provide a realistic interpretation of respective axioms, usual in economics and data envelopment analysis (DEA), that otherwise seem to be unrealistic in many cases of production management and industrial engineering.

In addition to the potential conflict with reality and environmental objectives, there is a further objection against generic technological disposability axioms, namely that they are often not necessary in order to determine the (in)efficiency of production activities. We will consider this in Section 3.2.3.

---

[12]   http://www.bine.info/fileadmin/content/Publikationen/Themen-Infos/II_2010/BMWi_COO RETEC_Strategie_Deu.pdf: German Administration for Economy and Technology: Empfehlungen des COORETEC-Beirats zur Förderung von Forschung und Entwicklung CO_2-emissionsarmer Kraftwerkstechnologien und CO_2-Abscheide-und Speichertechnologien. Berlin 2009, p. 7.

2.4.2 Rationality of Inefficient Activities

In the preceding decade, several authors have analysed the question as to whether it can be rational to produce inefficiently (see, e.g., the seven papers in Fandel 2009). Corollaries 2.5 and 2.6 have shown, however, that this is impossible for those efficiency notions which are defined consistently for preferences without conflicts. Nevertheless, as Dyckhoff and Ahn (2001) already pointed out, one has to notice the fact that *efficiency is always relative in a double sense*, on the one hand regarding the set of compared alternatives and on the other regarding the set of considered objectives. The first kind of relativity is well known from traditional production theory: An inefficient production activity would become part of the efficient frontier of the PPS if all activities dominating it were no longer possible, e.g. because of a further resource constraint. Thus, it is the second kind of relativity – as characteristic of MCPT – that constitutes the discussion in the literature on 'rational inefficiencies' (pioneered by Bogetoft and Hougaard 2003): An inefficient activity may become efficient if the set of objectives is changed, e.g. if this activity is better than all other activities, dominating it before, regarding a further (e.g. environmental) objective to be added. The literature has discussed several kinds of such rational inefficiencies (Fandel 2009).

In their paper, Bogetoft and Hougaard (2003) pointed out that allowing for technical inefficiency may be rational from the perspective of an enterprise as DMU if the resulting slack of excess resources is valuable, at least to some degree. The following quote by Fandel and Lorth (2009, p. 410), commenting on the approach of Bogetoft and Hougaard (2003), describes exactly one of those decision situations which are considered here as different valuation modes or levels, eventually not being preferentially consistent:

> For this, the objective function is extended by slacks as additional components so that a production alternative that turns out to be efficient with respect to the objective function in a higher-dimensioned decision space does not need to be efficient in a subspace such as the producer's technical production possibilities set. Since input slacks are allocated a positive value, technical inefficiency itself becomes valuable and a trade-off evolves between gaining technical efficiency by reducing input levels and the consumption of positively valued slacks implying higher input levels and less technical efficiency.

In the terminology introduced before, one would write: The input of resources involves not only those costs according to the usual assumption A6a of traditional production theory, but furthermore other (opportunity) costs for not explicitly considered (future) production possibilities, i.e. not captured by the given PPS $\mathcal{P}$, which are also to be calculated against the revenues from the products generated with the actual resource input. Moreover, there may be valuable slacks not only on the input side of production, but on the output side, too. For example, large pieces, originally being trim loss of cutting materials such as paper or steel from stock, can be put into inventory for further cutting on future demand (Dyckhoff and Gehring 1988).

Even in cases of (short term) profit maximising as exclusive objective, Fandel and Lorth (2010) have discussed and demonstrated further reasons for technically inefficient profit maxima.[13] They conclude that (p. 424):

> a profit maximizing production may under certain economic circumstances imply technical inefficiency in the sense that the enterprise voluntarily employs a larger than technically necessary quantity of input in order to produce a given quantity of output. It turned out that those situations arise if the evaluation of inputs and outputs by the enterprise's objective function is non-monotonic as, for instance, in the case of input prices being not strictly positive over the entire domain and revenues being non-monotonic or fixed. The mechanism behind this result is quite simple: zero or negative prices in the 'right' region of the technology set allow the enterprise to realise production points away from the efficient boundary of its technology set as they enable constant or even increasing values of the objective (profit) function if, for example, the input quantity increases for a given output level. Furthermore, we have discussed some non-pathological real life situations in which non-positive prices may occur. They are rare but they exist.

As such real-life situations, Fandel and Lorth (2010) discuss markets for (undesirable) by-products, energy markets, all-units quantity discounts as well as wage concessions. In any case, a non-monotonic evaluation is crucial for the existence of a technically inefficient profit maximum, as Corollary 2.5 has stated for more general instances. Then, the rationality concepts of technical efficiency on the first (lower) level and of the profit maximum on the second (higher) level are preferentially inconsistent.

2.4.3 Further Insights, Application Areas and Limitations

Multi-criteria production theory (MCPT) is a generalisation of traditional production theories. In the way that traditional theories lay the foundations for cost and revenue theories, MCPT can be utilised to expand knowledge on the theory and practice of performance evaluation in general. This is of major importance with distinct conflicting objectives which cannot easily be made commensurable by financial terms, a fact regularly occurring in production management and industrial engineering, particularly with sustainability evaluations. Important further insights of MCPT are:

• Some fundamental premises of traditional production theory, usually not scrutinised, can be questioned and answered more systematically and in a more profound way, using the knowledge and know-how of decision theory. This holds

---

[13] While proposing possible future research directions, Avkiran and Parker (2010, p. 4) stated that "the notion of rationalizing inefficiency measured by DEA has not received significant attention."

especially true for the following questions: What are the relevant inputs and outputs of a production system to be modelled in accordance with the production manager's perception of reality and preferences, in order to explain his or her behaviour? Which are relevant for the performance evaluation by an external evaluator?[14]

- The efficiency of production is relative in a double sense, namely, on the one hand, regarding the production possibility set (PPS) as a set of compared decision alternatives and, on the other hand, regarding the set of relevant objectives as decision or evaluation criteria to be considered.

- The characterisation of activities as 'efficient' or 'inefficient' on different valuation levels depends strongly on the consistency and the monotonicity of the values between these levels.

MCPT generalises traditional theories in such a way that all their propositions and methods remain valid for the special cases considered before. The frontiers of fundamental theories and concepts underlying methods and techniques, particularly those of performance analysis, in various fields of production management, industrial engineering, and sustainability analysis are thus expanded. The generalisation is achieved by a synthesis of both production and decision theory such that MCPT offers fruitful insights into various problems discussed in the recent literature. Some of them are considered in this book. Amongst other such topics are the definition and selection of relevant inputs and outputs, proper efficiency measurement models for undesirable products and factors, as well as the rationality of inefficient production.

The essential advantage of MCPT is that it allows strictly differentiating technological from non-technological assumptions, i.e. those concerning the actual (inputs and outputs of the considered) transformation process, such as the returns to scale from production, from those of value impact aspects, such as nonlinear market responses, e.g. in the case of monopolistic actors. Therefore, MCPT enables us to clearly distinguish between the possible production activities under the full control of a decision-making unit (i.e. the PPS) versus their consequences for markets and other economic, social, or ecological environments, modelled by multiple value functions.

On the one hand, the technological inputs and outputs of a production system are usually more easily observable and measurable than the state of the fundamental

---

[14] For example, with respect to the pitfalls in selecting inputs and outputs in data envelopment analysis (DEA), Dyson et al. (2001, p. 248) suggest a protocol where any performance measures may be eliminated "that are not strongly related to the objectives of the organization. This might be achieved by a careful consideration of the consistency of the mission, objectives and performance measures." Such a consideration is, however, the genuine part of a performance measurement methodology based on MCPT (Afsharian et al. 2016).

goals, which are actually the ultimate focus of interest. On the other hand, performance criteria should ideally represent fundamental values as much as possible. However, meaningful estimations of the performance of a production system are often still possible as long as the inputs and outputs as well as the benefits and costs are chosen as a means to an end in compatibility with the fundamental objectives. The more the benefits and costs represent the fundamental goals, the better (i.e. the sharper) the performance ratings are (cf. Sect. 3.4). However, benefits and costs of production essentially depend on its inputs and outputs whose technological interdependence has thus to be taken account of carefully in any performance analysis of production management and industrial engineering. It may be of particular interest for future research how MCPT can be made useful for the frontier-based performance analysis of supply chains as complex multi-stage production systems (cf. e.g. the respective review of Agrell and Hatami-Marbini 2013).

However, it is important for fruitful applications of MCPT that the assumptions about the technological nature of the PPS and about the preference assessing features of the VPS are of such a kind that they are realistic as well as helpful for implementing useful methods of production management or performance analysis in practice. Since the usefulness of specific technological properties of the PPS is well known from traditional production theories, we will concentrate on the influence of different features of linear value functions in this book.

References

Afsharian M, Ahn H, Neumann L (2016) Generalized DEA – An approach for supporting input/output factor determination in DEA. Benchmarking: An International Journal 23:1892–1909

Agrell PJ, Hatami-Marbini A (2013) Frontier-based performance analysis models for supply chain management: State of the art and research directions. Computers & Industrial Engineering 66:567–583

Avkiran NK, Parker BR (2010) Pushing the DEA research envelope. Socio-Economic Planning Sciences 44:1–7

Baumgärtner S, Dyckhoff H, Faber M, Proops J, Schiller J (2001) The concept of joint production and ecological economics. Ecological Economics 36:365–372

Bogetoft P, Hougaard JL (2003) Rational inefficiencies. Journal of Productivity Analysis 20:243–271

Dakpo KH, Jeanneaux P, Latruffe L (2016) Modelling pollution-generating technologies in performance benchmarking: Recent developments, limits and future prospects in the nonparametric framework. European Journal of Operational Research 250:347–359

Dano S (1966) Industrial Production Models. Springer, Wien/New York

Dinkelbach W, Rosenberg O (2004) Erfolgs- und umweltorientierte Produktionstheorie. 5th ed, Springer, Berlin et al.

Dyckhoff H (1992) Betriebliche Produktion: Theoretische Grundlagen einer umweltorientierten Produktionswirtschaft. Springer, Berlin et al.

Dyckhoff H (2003) Neukonzeption der Produktionstheorie. Zeitschrift für Betriebswirtschaft 73:705–732

Dyckhoff H (2018) Multi-criteria production theory: Foundation of non-financial and sustainability performance evaluation. Journal of Business Economics 88:851–882 (DOI: 10.1007/s11573-017-0885-1; open access)

Dyckhoff H (2019) Multi-criteria production theory: Convexity propositions and reasonable axioms. Journal of Business Economics 89:719–735

Dyckhoff H, Ahn H (2001) Sicherstellung der Effektivität und Effizienz der Führung als Kernfunktion des Controlling. Kostenrechnungspraxis 45:111–121

Dyckhoff H, Ahn H (2010) Verallgemeinerte DEA-Modelle zur Performanceanalyse. Zeitschrift für Betriebswirtschaft 80:1249–1276

Dyckhoff H, Allen K (2001) Measuring ecological efficiency with Data Envelopment Analysis (DEA). European Journal of Operational Research 132:312–325

Dyckhoff H, Gehring H (1988) Trim loss and inventory planning in a small textile firm. In: Fandel G, Dyckhoff H, Reese J (ed): Essays on Production Theory and Planning. Springer, Berlin/Heidelberg, pp 181–190

Dyckhoff H, Spengler T (2010) Produktionswirtschaft. 3rd ed, Springer, Berlin et al.

Dyson RG, Allen R, Camanho AS, Podinovski VV, Sarrico CC, Shale EA (2001) Pitfalls and protocols in DEA. European Journal of Operational Research 132:245–259

Eisenführ F, Weber M, Langer T (2010) Rational Decision Making. Springer, Berlin et al.

Esser J (2001) Entscheidungstheoretische Erweiterung der Produktionstheorie. Peter Lang, Frankfurt a. M.

Fandel G (2009) (ed) Rational Inefficiencies. Zeitschrift für Betriebswirtschaft, Special Issue 4/2009. Gabler, Wiesbaden

Fandel G (2010) Produktions- und Kostentheorie. 8th ed, Springer, Berlin et al.

Fandel G, Lorth M (2009) On the technical (in)efficiency of a profit maximum. International Journal of Production Economics 121:409–426

Fandel G, Lorth M (2010) Technische Ineffizienz als Ergebnis rationalen Entscheidungsverhaltens. Zeitschrift für Betriebswirtschaft 80:477–494

Färe R, Grosskopf S (1996) Intertemporal Production Frontiers: With Dynamic DEA. Kluwer, Boston et al.

Frisch R (1965) Theory of Production. D. Reidel Publ., Dordrecht

Gutenberg E (1951) Grundlagen der Betriebswirtschaftslehre. Band I: Die Produktion. 24th ed, 1983, Springer, Berlin

Hasenkamp G (1992) Multiple objectives in the theory of the firm. Journal of Productivity Analysis 3:323–335

Koopmans TC (1951) Analysis of production as an efficient combination of activities. In: Koopmans TC (ed) Activity Analysis of Production and Allocation. J. Wiley & Sons, New York, pp 33–97

Kuosmanen T, Kortelainen M (2005) Measuring eco-efficiency of production with Data Envelopment Analysis. Journal of Industrial Ecology 9:59–72

Liu W, Meng W, Li X, Zhang DQ (2010) DEA models with undesirable inputs and outputs. Annals of Operations Research 173:177–194

Myhre G, Shindell D, Bréon F-M, Collins W, Fuglestvedt J, Huang J, Koch D, Lamarque J-F, Lee D, Mendoza B, Nakajima T, Robock A, Stephens G, Takemura T, Zhang H (2013): Anthropogenic and Natural Radiative Forcing. In: Change Stocker, TF, Qin D, Plattner G-K, Tignor M, Allen SK, Boschung J, Nauels A, Xia Y, Bex V, Midgley PM (eds.): Climate Change 2013: The Physical Science Basis. Contribution of Working Group I to the Fifth Assessment Report of the Intergovernmental Panel on Climate. Cambridge University Press, Cambridge/New York, pp 659–740

Shephard RW (1970) Theory of Cost and Production Functions. Princeton Univ. Press, Princeton NJ

Souren R (1996) Theorie betrieblicher Reduktion. Physica, Heidelberg

Wojcik V, Dyckhoff H, Gutgesell S (2017) The desirable input of undesirable factors in Data Envelopment Analysis. Annals of Operations Research 259:461–484

Chapter 3
Data Envelopment Methodology of Performance Evaluation[1]

Abstract. Chapter 1 has explained why the measurement of effectiveness and efficiency constitutes the core of performance evaluation. While traditional methods of cost/benefit-analysis and management accounting usually measure the performance of activities in monetary terms, data envelopment analysis (DEA) is an important methodology of performance evaluation for activities which are characterised by non-financial data. Chapter 3 uses results of Chapter 2 regarding multi-criteria production theory (MCPT) for linear value functions in order to form a firm foundation of DEA by generalising its common methodology. This generalisation strictly distinguishes between inputs and outputs as basic technological entities on the one hand, respectively costs and benefits as preferentially determined (in general non-financial) performance attributes on the other hand. At first, the relations between DEA and MCPT are explained as well as the question is critically discussed what kind of data may be enveloped by a linear or convex hull. The next three sections analyse the properties of well-known radial and additive DEA models and their systematic generalisations with respect to linear value functions of increasing complexity.

Keywords Data envelopment analysis • Efficiency measurement • Generalised cost/benefit-analysis • Model selection

---

[1] Parts of Sections 3.1, 3.3 and 3.4 are adapted from Dyckhoff (2018) by permission of the author. Section 3.1.2 is a revised and extended translation of parts from Dyckhoff and Ahn (2010) by permission of Springer Nature. Sections 3.2.1 and 3.2.2 are largely taken from Wojcik, Dyckhoff and Gutgesell (2019) by permission of the authors. Section 3.2.3 is adapted from Dyckhoff (2019) by permission of Springer Nature.

47

3.1   Data Envelopment and Multi-criteria Performance Analysis

Non-financial performance evaluation is characterised by the fact that at least one relevant performance criterion is not measured in monetary terms and therefore cannot easily be aggregated with the other relevant criteria into a single measure of overall performance (cf. Sect. 1.1). Hence, multiple performance criteria have to be considered which are *a priori* incommensurable. Non-financial performance evaluation may therefore be looked at as an application field of multi-criteria decision making (MCDM) and multi-attribute utility theory (MAUT). In regard to an important *methodology of performance evaluation*, Wallenius et al. (2008, pp. 1337 and 1343) state in the outlines of interesting future research questions of their seminal review of MCDM and MAUT already more than a decade ago:[2]

> Data envelopment analysis (DEA) has grown in importance and its relationship with multiple objective linear programming (MOLP) has been explored. (...) Of course, DEA and MOLP usually have different purposes: DEA is used for performance measurement, whereas MOLP is used for decision aiding choice. The observation about the structural similarity between DEA and MOLP has sparked synergistic advances in both models. (...) MOLP models can be used to generate novel ways of incorporating a decision maker's preferences into DEA.

What DEA and MOLP have in common is that they both try to model good decisions. However, as a rule, DEA is used descriptively with empirical data and – in contrast – MOLP prescriptively with forecasted data. The structural similarity of DEA and MOLP has been disclosed by Joro et al. (1998) and utilised by Halme et al. (1999) to incorporate preference information into DEA (cf. Joro and Korhonen 2015 for a comprehensive presentation). Nevertheless, there is a fundamental difference between DEA and MOLP, because the latter makes no systematic use of the technological concept **production possibility set** (PPS) and its essential properties, e.g. the returns to scale from production. Three characteristics of DEA, which are at the same time untypical of MOLP, are:

1. envelopment of (measured) data,
2. interpretation of the data as consequences of production activities of decision-making units (DMUs), whereby

---

[2] The difference between the purposes 'performance measurement' and 'decision aiding choice' – asserted in this quotation – is not convincing because performance measurement is not an ultimate purpose but a means to some end. Actually, from the usual perspective of management accounting and control, performance measurement is an instrument mainly used for two ultimate purposes with typically conflicting results, namely either *decision facilitating and aiding* in the case of one decision maker or one team, or else *decision influencing and control* in principal/agent-situations with asymmetrically distributed information and opportunistic agents (Demski and Feltham 1976).

3. the envelopment is based on exogenous knowledge about the underlying production technology.

DEA is thus a methodology for "measuring efficiency of decision-making units" (Charnes et al. 1978) and its concept draws much on *production theory* (Charnes et al. 1985). This may be one reason why MOLP and DEA have developed separately so far during the last forty years, despite several attempts to integrate DEA with MCDM (Belton 1992; Doyle and Green 1993; Joro et al. 1998). In fact, DEA draws much on *decision theory* as well, even though this aspect has been widely ignored in the DEA literature.

3.1.1 *Generalisation of DEA by MCPT*

An exception can be found in a methodological review on "DEA: Prior to choosing a model" by Cook et al. (2014). With respect to the crucial question of selecting and defining the inputs and outputs which are relevant for the performance evaluation at hand, they state (p. 2):

> In summary, if the underlying DEA problem represents a form of 'production process', then 'inputs' and 'outputs' can often be more clearly identified. The resources used or required are usually the inputs and the outcomes are the outputs.
>
> If, however, the DEA problem is a general benchmarking problem, then the inputs are usually the 'less-the-better' type of performance measures and the outputs (...) the 'more the-better' type (...). DEA then can be viewed as a multiple-criteria evaluation methodology where DMUs are alternatives, and the DEA inputs and outputs are two sets of performance criteria where one set (inputs) is to be minimized and the other (outputs) to be maximized.

Each of these two alternatives and unconnected perspectives has its own difficulties. This can be illustrated by the example of cement plants of Sections 2.1.2 and 2.3.1.

Example 3.1: Inconsistent and problematic definitions of inputs and outputs

Assume a decision maker examines the sustainability of certain production units, such as cement plants which use the factor labour and produce undesired emissions (cf. Example 2.1):

a) On the one hand, cement factories unambiguously constitute production processes with labour as a resource and carbon dioxide as an emission. Following Cook et al.'s (2014) above mentioned first DEA perspective, labour and CO_2 are therefore to be identified as input to be minimised, and output to be maximised, respectively. Indeed, in the (economic) view of the shareholders of the firm, the input of labour does imply wage costs to be minimised. Contrarily, social and ecological objectives of other stakeholders, such as trade unions or future generations, usually call for the opposite optimisation directions, namely the maximisation of workers' employment and the minimisation of climate change caused by CO_2 outcome.

b) On the other hand, Cook et al.'s (2014) second perspective considers DEA simply as a "multiple-criteria evaluation methodology" where the output CO_2 – to be minimised for ecological reasons – needs to be re-defined as an 'input', which is hardly justifiable from a production-theoretical point of view. In particular, it contradicts the definition of Frisch (1965, p. 8), cited in Section 2.1.1. Moreover, being a performance measure to be maximised, the profit of the cement factory would be treated as an 'output' by DEA. However, this can lead to unrealistic properties and results, particularly regarding the assumed returns to scale from production, for example when the cement firm has a monopoly on its local market (see Example 2.3).

Multi-criteria production theory (MCPT), presented in Chapter 2, tells us, however, that the two perspectives of 'production process' versus 'benchmarking problem' in the quotation of Cook et al. (2014) are in fact not mutually exclusive, but instead represent two sides of the same coin. The value functions (2.1) of Example 2.1 of cement plants illustrate how the problem of correctly defining the inputs and outputs in DEA can be resolved. The crucial point is not whether either production theory or else decision theory are alternative theoretical foundations of DEA, but rather how to form an adequate synthesis of both theories.

Literature overview: Until now, there seems to be only a few papers in the DEA literature dealing with such a synthesised approach:

• Dyckhoff and Allen (2001) developed the first systematic approach for deriving (ecologically) generalised DEA models according to MCPT. Starting from well-known assumptions of DEA and activity analysis, they differentiate four specific kinds of partial preference relations with respect to the input/output-vectors of the production activities: (a) the *classical case* where all inputs and outputs are goods; (b) the *standard case* of environmental economics with goods and bads as outputs as well as inputs; (c) the *CML case* (of the Institute of Environmental Sciences of Leiden University) with ecological categories as objectives, e.g. global warming, which are measured by (linear) impact functions of the inputs and outputs; and (d) the *general linear case* of multiple value functions. We will investigate cases (a), (b) and (d) in Sections 3.2 to 3.4.

• By referring to the CML case (c) of Dyckhoff and Allen (2001) in a short footnote, Kuosmanen and Kortelainen (2005) proposed a similar approach of using environmental impact (or pressure) categories in DEA. They examine how DEA can be adapted for this purpose. Their reasoning is that DEA accounts for substitution possibilities between different natural resources and emissions and does not require subjective judgement about the weights although soft weight restrictions can be incorporated. Finally, they use their approach to assess the eco-efficiency of road transportation in three Finnish towns. We will consider such ecological performance evaluations in Section 3.4 as well as in Chapter 4.

• Dyckhoff and Ahn (2010) refine the generalised DEA approach proposed by Dyckhoff and Allen (2001). They distinguish the multiple value functions into the two categories of cost (or 'effort') and of benefit functions. Furthermore, they demonstrate how the most widely used, radial DEA models can be derived from MCPT (shown in our next Sections from 3.1.2 to 3.2).

The results for general linear cost and benefit functions are illustrated by the example of cement plants. Finally, they discuss the need for a comprehensive methodology extending the pure generalisation of the mathematical DEA models to an advanced DEA performance evaluation conception.

- Afsharian et al. (2016) pick up their suggestion and propose such an advanced DEA approach for the particular purpose of determining the relevant performance criteria. It is exemplified by the case of measuring pharma stores' efficiency concerning their goal of customer retention. The three steps of the procedure of Afsharian et al. include the development of a system of objectives, the derivation of corresponding performance criteria (as inputs and outputs) as well as the construction of associated cost and benefit functions. This approach is intended to contribute to solving the following problems: (a) selecting the relevant inputs and outputs, (b) handling objects with dual roles as input or output, (c) undesirable objects.
- A survey by Wojcik et al. (2017) of the DEA literature on bads reveals that only 22 (of 345) articles explicitly address the (desirable) input of such undesirable objects into the first stage of a single- or multi-stage process. And only four of them consider a real application with those original factors, all of which are waste water. A detailed analysis shows that all current approaches are based on two core ideas involving various efficiency measures. Disposability assumptions, otherwise common in DEA – and in economics –, are rarely used, presumably because the modelled processes are disposal processes. Regarding the standard case (b) of environmental economics defined by Dyckhoff and Allen (2001), the authors finally demonstrate in an example how DEA models with bads as inputs (and outputs) can be systematically derived from MCPT. Section 3.3 will demonstrate this here.
- A comprehensive, detailed framework for advanced DEA based on MCPT – asked for by Dyckhoff and Ahn (2010) – has been developed and published (in German) by Wojcik (2018). It guides the user through a well-founded selection of indicators as well as through the reasonable choice of proper DEA model characteristics. We will refer to it only, namely in Section 4.5 of our book, which instead focusses on the theoretical and methodical foundations of non-financial performance evaluation. For practical applications, the book of Wojcik (2018) is recommended strongly as a further reading.

The generalisation of DEA by MCPT throws light on some of the open questions in DEA "prior to choosing a model" (Cook et al. 2014) as well as in respect of interpreting the results of performance analyses obtained with such models. A central question is concerned with the kind of data that is to be enveloped.

3.1.2 What Kind of Data May Be Enveloped?

Having been researched for forty years, DEA still appears to be an ever-growing field. The various data bases of the Web of Science exhibit *more than fifteen thousand publications* for the topic 'data envelopment analysis', with more than fifteen hundred entries for the year 2018 alone. Their majority includes numerical application examples, often with real data. However, as a rule, these are at most demonstrations of the feasibility of new DEA model variants in practical questions without any further empirical validation. Evidence that DEA is used routinely for the performance analysis in reality is scarce. That is quite surprising because relevant textbooks of internationally recognised experts exist already for a long time (e.g. Färe et al. 1994, Coelli et al. 2005, Cooper et al. 2007, Thanassoulis et al. 2008 or Zhu 2015). Beyond that, there is a broad range of – partly even publicly – available DEA software (Barr 2004). The main reason for the restraint of real applications lies probably rather in the methodical complexity and in the resulting problems of the data acquisition, aggregation and interpretation. In each of these three phases the DEA user is exposed to a number of pitfalls that can considerably affect the validity of the results (Dyson et al. 2001).

A central question is the *selection of the DEA model* variant on which an application should be based. That is to say, the results of the performance analysis depend essentially on this selection, as Wojcik et al. (2019) demonstrate for the exemplary case of a welfare evaluation of 27 states of the European Union. It will be illustrated here in Sections 3.2.1 and 3.2.2 with a simple numerical example (cf. already Sect. 1.2.2). In particular, the question to what extent the data may be enveloped plays a decisive role, as does the orientation of the efficiency measure in the case of radial DEA models. Both imply certain assumptions about the type of performance measurement as well as about the actual possibilities of the DMUs $j = 1, ..., n$ to be evaluated. The empirical validity of these (often implicit) assumptions is rarely reflected in more detail in the DEA literature. The question how to justify a certain selection of DEA model features arises to an even greater extent if DEA is to be placed on a solid theoretical foundation with the help of MCPT.

In order to analyse this question, we start with the usual justification of DEA. It refers to the pioneer contribution of Charnes et al. (1978) in which they introduce and motivate DEA on the basis of economic categories. Though, instead of applying DEA to inputs x and outputs y, we transfer and generalise their approach to the multiple, nonnegative costs c and benefits b known from Section 2.1.1. This coincides with their original approach if the special ('classical') case A6a, defined in Section 2.2.1, is assumed, where costs and benefits are identical with certain inputs and outputs, i.e. $c = x$ and $b = y$.

Charnes et al. (1978) suppose that, in principle, nonnegative weighting factors $v = (v_1, ..., v_k)$ and $\mu = (\mu_1, ..., \mu_\ell)$ exist for all relevant (in general non-monetary) cost types $\kappa = 1, ..., k$ and benefit types $\beta = 1, ..., \ell$ of the observed activities, but that these are initially unknown (and have later to be determined individually for each DMU). The factors $v = (v_1, ..., v_k)$ shall make it possible to map the different costs on one and the same, uniform ratio scale such that they are comparable with each other. By the weighted sum

$$C(v;c) = v \cdot c = \sum_{\kappa=1}^{k} v_\kappa c_\kappa \in \mathbb{R}_+ \tag{3.1}$$

the *total costs* are evaluated in this way on the basis of a virtual value scale (usually called 'virtual input' in DEA literature), which may even be monetary in particular instances. The linear aggregation (3.1) shall hold analogously for the weighting of the different benefits. Thus, the weighted sum of the individual benefits

$$B(\boldsymbol{\mu};\boldsymbol{b}) = \boldsymbol{\mu} \cdot \boldsymbol{b} = \sum_{\beta=1}^{\ell} \mu_\beta b_\beta \in \mathbb{R}_+ \tag{3.2}$$

measures the *total benefit* on a certain scale. Thereby, the virtual scales for total cost and total benefit can be different. Therefore, the difference of both virtual values cannot reasonably be calculated, their quotient admittedly instead:

$$\Theta := \frac{B}{C} = \frac{\boldsymbol{\mu} \cdot \boldsymbol{b}}{\boldsymbol{v} \cdot \boldsymbol{c}} = \frac{\sum_{\beta=1}^{\ell} \mu_\beta b_\beta}{\sum_{\kappa=1}^{k} v_\kappa c_\kappa} \tag{3.3}$$

This quotient corresponds to a benefit-effectiveness of the costs and thus characterises the *(value) productivity* of the considered activity in an aggregated way as a one-dimensional indicator. Here, an activity with inputs and outputs $\boldsymbol{z} = (\boldsymbol{x}, \boldsymbol{y})$ is fully determined by its values $\boldsymbol{v} = (\boldsymbol{c}, \boldsymbol{b})$. The indicator Θ can be interpreted as a performance measure of the activity which indicates the extent to which benefits arise in relation to costs when inputs are transformed into outputs.

The units of measurement of both virtual ratio scales – as for ratio scales in general – are only determined up to one multiplicative constant each. Therefore, two degrees of freedom exist in the numerical determination. As a first step of *normalisation*, it is possible to restrict the (nonnegative) quotient of virtual benefits and costs by a finite upper bound, e.g. by one (or 100%), provided that the benefits are limited upwards in relation to the costs of the activities in question. Hence, without loss of generality, we obtain a normalised performance value, usually called *efficiency score*: $0 \leq \Theta \leq 1$.

In order to calculate the numerical value of the efficiency score Θ_j of an activity j with the value vector $\boldsymbol{v}_j = (\boldsymbol{c}_j; \boldsymbol{b}_j)$, however, the weights $\boldsymbol{v}$ and $\boldsymbol{\mu}$ do not only have to exist, but, moreover, have to be known explicitly.

The fundamentally new idea of the so-called **CCR model** by Charnes, Cooper and Rhodes (1978) was that the weightings of the individual inputs and outputs – in our generalised case the weightings of the (usually non-monetary) costs and benefits – should not be determined in a single calculation as weights equal for all DMUs. Rather, each DMU j may chose its own, individually most favourable cost and benefit factors $\boldsymbol{v}_j$ and $\boldsymbol{\mu}_j$, that put it 'in the best light', however, under the condition that these factors then simultaneously also apply to the other DMUs and that the above mentioned normalisation holds for every DMU. Formally, for each DMU[3] $o \in \{1, \dots, n\}$ the following *quotient programme* as nonlinear optimisation model has to be solved:[4]

$$\Theta_o^* = \max_{v \geq 0, \mu \geq 0} \Theta_o \text{ such that } \Theta_j \leq 1 \text{ for } j = 1, \dots, n \tag{3.4}$$

Mathematically, the normalisation of the efficiency scores as optimisation constraint for all DMUs implies for the quotient (3.3):[5]

$$B - 1 \cdot C = \sum_{\beta=1}^{\ell} \mu_\beta b_\beta - \sum_{\kappa=1}^{k} v_\kappa c_\kappa \leq 0$$

Since the normalisation constraints of (3.4) employ only one of the two degrees of freedom in the choice of the units of the two ratio scales, the quotient programme (3.4) can be transformed into a linear optimisation task for each DMU $o \in \{1, \dots, n\}$, known as the **multiplier form** in DEA, by means of a further determination of the cost factors according to $C_o = 1$ by a second normalisation step, which may be different for each DMU $o \in \{1, \dots, n\}$ as result of the *n linear (optimisation) programmes*:

$$\Theta_o^* = \max_{v \geq 0, \mu \geq 0} B_o = \mu b_o$$
$$\text{such that } v c_o = 1 \text{ and } \mu b_j - v c_j \leq 0 \text{ for } j = 1, \dots, n \tag{3.5}$$

According to the duality theory of linear programming (LP), the following optimisation task is equivalent to (3.5) and known in DEA literature as the **envelopment form**, with $\lambda = (\lambda_1, \dots, \lambda_n)$:

$$\theta_o^* = \min_{\lambda \geq 0} \theta_o \text{ such that } \sum_{j=1}^{n} \lambda_j b_j \geq b_o \text{ and } \sum_{j=1}^{n} \lambda_j c_j \leq \theta_o c_o \tag{3.6}$$

Duality theory states: $\Theta_o^* = \theta_o^*$, and the optimal solutions of the primary variables of one linear programme, i.e. v_o^*, μ_o^* for the multiplier form and λ_o^* for the envelopment form, are identical to the optimal values of the dual variables of the other linear programme. Hence, it is sufficient to solve one of the two programmes.

---

[3] In line with DEA literature the index o is used here instead of j to indicate the variable to be optimised. Since in DEA all DMUs once represent the unit to be optimised – and in the other cases the units for comparison – the index o varies analogously to the index j from 1 to n.

[4] In order to avoid inefficient or weakly efficient solutions, which can result from weightings of individual costs and benefits with a zero value, only strictly positive weightings $v > 0$ und $\mu > 0$ should actually be permitted. Since such open intervals of the optimisation variables in general do not lead to an (achievable) maximum – but possibly to a (arbitrarily approximated) supremum only – DEA usually avoids potential inefficient solutions by some modifications or extensions of the calculations. This will be further discussed in Section 3.2.2.

[5] It should be noted that though this difference between the virtual benefits and costs is thus numerically limited by zero, this difference does not have to make sense at all, i.e. it cannot easily be interpreted as profit, since benefits and costs can still be measured in different units (the factor '1' is not dimensionless in this case)!

The model in envelopment form can be interpreted as follows: For the considered DMU the costs are to be reduced proportionally as far as possible, namely as long as the values of the DMU modified in this manner are dominated by some nonnegative linear combination of the c/b-vectors of all DMUs, i.e. by such a linear combination of values which on the one hand still exhibits at least as much benefits as DMU o and on the other hand at most as much proportionally reduced costs. Therefore, following the terminology of the so-called 'input-oriented' models of traditional DEA, the two above LP models can analogously be named as *cost-oriented (basic) radial DEA models of* the (thus generalised) *CCR type*.

Analogously, an alternative second normalisation step by determining the benefit factors according to $B_o = 1$ within each of the n nonlinear quotient programmes (3.4) leads to the two *benefit-oriented (basic) radial DEA models of CCR type*, namely the corresponding *multiplier form*:

$$\frac{1}{\Theta_o^*} = \eta_o^* = \min_{v \geq 0, \mu \geq 0} C_o = vc_o \tag{3.7}$$

such that $\mu b_o = 1$ and $\mu b_j - vc_j \leq 0$ for $j = 1, ..., n$

and the *envelopment form* as its dual linear programme:

$$\eta_o^* = \max_{\lambda \geq 0} \eta_o \text{ such that } \sum_{j=1}^n \lambda_j b_j \geq \eta_o b_o \text{ and } \sum_{j=1}^n \lambda_j c_j \leq c_o \tag{3.8}$$

All four variants (3.5) to (3.8) are equivalent in the sense that they use the same cost and benefit data $v_j = (c_j; b_j)$ and that the performance scores calculated by them are identical. Syntactically, these models conform to those of traditional DEA (simply by replacing the symbols for costs and benefits with those for the inputs and outputs: $c \to x$ und $b \to y$). Semantically, though, the above LP models are fundamentally different from the well-known traditional DEA models, unless for the special case where the costs are measured by the inputs and the benefits by the outputs – as easily to determine proxy indicators for real costs and benefits. This 'classical case' – according to which $c = x$ and $b = y$ (as per A6a from Section 2.2.1) – will be discussed in Section 3.2. The main semantical (not formal) discrepancy to the generalisation of DEA by MCPT will then become clear in the following Sections 3.3 to 3.5 for more general (linear) cost and benefit functions $c(x, y)$ and $b(x, y)$.

3.1.3 Justification of Traditional DEA

In general, the observed costs c_j and benefits b_j of the considered DMUs $j = 1, ..., n$ do not depend on the inputs x_j and outputs y_j in the simple way of the classical case A6a. It has to be very clear that the above justification of the linear envelopment of the cost and benefit data in models (3.6) and (3.8) by duality theory (following Charnes et al. 1978) has nothing to do with the actual production possibilities of the DMUs! Rather, this *linear envelope of the costs and benefits* of the DMUs is based on implicit assumptions about the underlying performance preferences which are made by the above derivation of the quotient programme (3.4) if it should be empirically valid.

That is to say, the precondition of the existence of the two sets of *fixed* weighting factors $\boldsymbol{v} = (v_1, \dots, v_k)$ and $\boldsymbol{\mu} = (\mu_1, \dots, \mu_\ell)$ in Section 3.1.2 – that can each be linked linearly to an identical value ratio scale in accordance with (3.1) and (3.2) – already presumes a corresponding linearity of the preferences of the decision maker or of the performance evaluator regarding the various cost types $\kappa = 1, \dots, k$ on the one hand as well as the benefit types $\beta = 1, \dots, \ell$ on the other hand. This becomes obvious by the fact that any multiplication of either all costs or else all benefits or of both with the same factor leads to the same overall performance rating of the DMUs if measured by the quotient (3.3). Therefore, such a performance measurement is indifferent to such changes. The numerical example already known from Section 2.3 serves as an illustration.

Example 3.2: Linear preferences concerning costs and benefits (cf. Example 2.2)
Let input and output $\boldsymbol{z} = (x; y)$ of three DMUs be given by $\boldsymbol{z}_A = (4; 2)$, $\boldsymbol{z}_B = (12; 3)$, and $\boldsymbol{z}_C = (18; 9)$, a cost function by $c(x; y) = x$ and a benefit function by $b(x; y) = y(10 - y)$. In contrast to the prior Figures 2.3 and 2.4, no assumption concerning further production possibilities is made. Therefore, only the three production activities A, B, and C exist below-left in the two-dimensional coordinate system of Figure 3.1. Cost and benefit are displayed to the right and above. The points $\tilde{A}$, $\tilde{B}$, and $\tilde{C}$ in value space (above-right) with $\boldsymbol{v}_A = (4; 16)$, $\boldsymbol{v}_B = (12; 21)$, and $\boldsymbol{v}_C = (18; 9)$ build the images $\boldsymbol{v} = (c; b)$ of the three production activities. We will demonstrate next that the assumptions in connection with (3.1), (3.2) and (3.3) – underlying the performance evaluation approach of Charnes et al. (1978) – presuppose indifference curves for the preferences which are identical with rays from the origin through any point in the above-right diagram. Figure 3.1 shows the corresponding rays as straight lines through the three value images $\tilde{A}$, $\tilde{B}$, and $\tilde{C}$.

The overall performance of a DMU is the better the steeper the line through its image point in value space. This holds because the weighting factors μ und ν in the corresponding quotient programme (3.4) are one-dimensional and because the quotients $\Theta_j = \mu b_j / \nu c_j$ are multiplied by the same single factor for all three DMUs j. The remaining quotient b_j / c_j equals the gradient of the ray through the value image of the DMU's activity. After normalisation according to quotient programme (3.4), point $\tilde{A}$, with a gradient of $16/4 = 4$ and a performance score $\Theta_A = 1$, belongs to the single DMU which is value efficient regarding the CCR model. The results of (3.4) for the two other DMUs are: $\Theta_B = (21/12)/4 = 7/16$ and $\Theta_C = (9/18)/4 = 1/8$. The cost oriented weights according to (3.5) are: $\mu_B = 1/48$, $v_B = 1/3$ as well as $\mu_C = 1/72$ and $v_C = 2/9$; the benefit oriented weights according to (3.7): $\mu_B = 1/21$, $v_B = 16/21$ as well as $\mu_C = 1/9$ and $v_C = 16/9$.

From the cost- and benefit-oriented envelopment variants (3.6) and (3.8) of the CCR model follows: The nonnegative linear combinations of $\tilde{A}$, $\tilde{B}$, and $\tilde{C}$ form a *polyhedric cone* in the value space of Figure 3.1 whose points can immediately be compared among each other regarding their performance, namely by the slope of the corresponding rays. Nevertheless, this does in no way imply that all these linear combinations of costs and benefits are in fact achievable by the considered DMUs.

Example 3.3 (2.3, 2.4 and 3.2 continued): Bounded revenue of monopolists
  Suppose that the three DMUs of Example 3.2 are the monopolists of Examples 2.3 or 2.4. Then, the maximum achievable revenue is bounded by 25 currency units (CU) because of the quadratic benefit function $b(x; y) = y(10 - y)$, irrespective of the actual production possibilities of the DMUs, as Figures 2.3 and 3.1 show. In contrast, the benefit-oriented CCR model (3.8) projects the inefficient value points $\tilde{B}$ and $\tilde{C}$ vertically upwards to their (so-called) *target points*

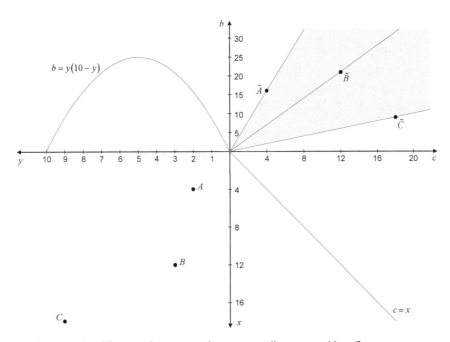

Fig. 3.1 Example of linear performance preferences regarding costs and benefits

(12; 48) and (18; 72) on the ray through the efficient point $\tilde{A}$. Thus, the *bench-marks* of 48 CU for the revenue of DMU B and of 72 CU for C, calculated by (3.8), are not achievable. This is similarly true for the cost-oriented CCR model (3.6) if at most convex combinations of the activities of the three DMUs would be possible, as is the case in Figure 2.3 where the whole ray through the value point $\tilde{A}$ is not achievable by such combinations, except for $\tilde{A}$ itself. Then, the cost-oriented target point of DMU C, calculated with (3.6), is (2.25; 9) with benchmarks for cost and input $c(x; y) = x$ of 2.25 that is smaller than the allowed minimum of 4 units.

Although the assumptions of Section 3.1.2 – generalising the approach of Charnes et al. (1978) – permit performance comparisons of all cost/benefit-vectors, these vectors are still hypothetical, in general. The presented approach does not allow to draw any conclusion about the fact which value points are actually realisable by production activities. For such an assertion one has to know the actual *production possibility set* (PPS) as well as the cost and benefit functions defined on it. Therefore, in order to state that certain value points are achievable by possible production activities one needs additional assumptions about the PPS $\mathcal{P}$ and the value function $v(z)$ introduced in Chapter 2.

Such additional assumptions, necessary for DEA, are typically in line with properties A1 and A7b of Sections 2.2.1 and 2.2.2. Then, the PPS is determined as a certain envelopment of the activities $z_j = (x_j, y_j)$ of the DMUs $j = 1, \dots, n$:

$$\mathcal{P} = \left\{ z = \sum_{j=1}^{n} \lambda_j z_j \middle| \lambda \in S \right\} \subset \mathbb{R}^{m+s} \quad \text{for} \quad S := \left\{ \lambda \in \mathbb{R}_+^n \middle| \tau_{min} \leq \sum_{j=1}^{n} \lambda_j \leq \tau_{max} \right\} \tag{3.9}$$

As known from Chapter 2, S defines the activity levels set with four cases of particular interest, determined by combining the two lower bounds $\tau_{min} \in \{0; 1\}$ with the two upper bounds $\tau_{max} \in \{1; \infty\}$. Each of the four different ranges for the activity levels λ_j implies a PPS $\mathcal{P}$ with either *variable* (VRS: 1;1), *non-increasing* (NIRS: 0;1), *non-decreasing* (NDRS: 1; ∞), or else *constant* (CRS: 0; ∞) *returns to scale*. Since these four types of PPS are all convex, and moreover are linear in the CRS case, we know from Theorem 2.1 of Section 2.2.2 that the corresponding *value possibility set* (VPS) $v(\mathcal{P}) \subset \mathbb{R}^{k+\ell}$ is convex (or linear), too, if the value function is *linear* according to A6c. The next proposition strengthens this assertion.

Theorem 3.1: If $v = v(z) = V \cdot z$ is a multi-dimensional linear value function (with value impact matrix V) defined on the inputs and outputs $z_j = (x_j; y_j) \in \mathbb{R}^{m+s}$ of a PPS of type

$$\mathcal{P} = \left\{ z = \sum_{j=1}^{n} \lambda_j z_j \middle| \lambda \in S \right\}$$

with the activity levels set $S \subset \mathbb{R}_+^n$, then, with $v_j := v(z_j) = V \cdot z_j \in \mathbb{R}^{k+\ell}$, the VPS has the same property in value space:

$$v(\mathcal{P}) = \left\{ v = \sum_{j=1}^n \lambda_j v_j \Big| \lambda \in S \right\}.$$

Proof: by simple algebraic transformations.

This theorem constitutes a further main proposition of multi-criteria production theory (MCPT) in addition to those of Chapter 2. *It is of fundamental importance for applications of DEA* since it states for linear value functions that the image of a convex (or linear) envelopment of activities in input/output-space equals the convex (respectively linear) envelopment of the image points of these activities in cost/benefit-space. Therefore, neither the explicit knowledge of the relevant inputs and outputs nor that of the respective linear value functions are necessary in order to determine the (value) efficiency scores of the DMUs. If the premises of Theorem 3.1 are true in an actual instance, it suffices to know the values of the relevant costs and benefits of the DMUs, only. Thus, Theorem 3.1 supplies a factual justification of the usual mathematical DEA models if they are applied directly to the costs and benefits instead of the inputs and outputs in such cases where the VPS has the same property (3.9) such as the PPS itself.

Hence, in connection with such types of convex or even linear PPS, the following sections of this chapter presuppose linear value functions, namely those of different degrees of complexity (in line with A6a, A6b, and A6c of Sect. 2.2). Furthermore, they concentrate on the envelopment form of DEA models and do not further discuss their multiplier form, which, in any case, can be received by building the corresponding dual LP model.[6]

3.2 DEA for the Classical Case of Goods

The simplest case of linear value functions – the *classical case* of production theory and DEA – is determined by $v(z) = z$, i.e. $c = x$ and $b = y$. Performance evaluation then considers as costs directly the inputs of relevant goods, respectively as benefits their outputs (cf. property A6a in Sect. 2.2.1). Often, DEA models are based on this assumption, but several models exist for other cases. However, which model fits best for a concrete performance evaluation also depends on suitable assumptions

---

[6] Such an extension would be beyond the scope of our brief book, which focusses on the foundation of non-financial performance analysis by MCPT instead. For comprehensive introductions to DEA cf. again Färe et al. (1994), Coelli et al. (2005), Cooper et al. (2007), Thanassoulis et al. (2008) or Zhu (2015).

concerning the shape of the PPS and of the VPS (in particular their convexity, additivity and returns to scale). Moreover, the model orientation as well as the distance metric of efficiency measurement affect the results, too.

3.2.1   Oriented Radial Performance Measurement

As before, let x_{ij} denote the quantity of the inputs $i = 1, ..., m$, y_{rj} that of the outputs $r = 1, ..., s$ and λ_j the activity level of the DMUs $j = 1, ..., n$. Then, the two variants (3.6) and (3.8) of the CCR model become:

Input-oriented CCR model (CCR-I) in envelopment form for goods

Minimise θ_o

such that $\sum_{j=1}^{n} \lambda_j \cdot x_{ij} \leq \theta_o \cdot x_{io}$ for $i = 1, ..., m$

$\qquad\qquad\qquad \sum_{j=1}^{n} \lambda_j \cdot y_{rj} \geq y_{ro}$ for $r = 1, ..., s$ (3.10)

$\qquad\qquad\qquad\qquad \lambda_j \geq 0$ for $j = 1, ..., n$

Output-oriented CCR model (CCR-O) in envelopment form for goods

Maximise η_o

such that $\sum_{j=1}^{n} \lambda_j \cdot x_{ij} \leq x_{io}$ for $i = 1, ..., m$

$\qquad\qquad\qquad \sum_{j=1}^{n} \lambda_j \cdot y_{rj} \geq \eta_o \cdot y_{ro}$ for $r = 1, ..., s$ (3.11)

$\qquad\qquad\qquad\qquad \lambda_j \geq 0$ for $j = 1, ..., n$

The value of the objective function of CCR-O model (3.11) as optimisation problem indicates the productivity factor η_o (greater than one) by which all outputs of the currently considered DMU o can be proportionately (i.e. radially) increased without decreasing the input. As a rule, we use its reciprocal value $\theta_o = 1/\eta_o$ instead, namely as an efficiency score between zero and one. For the CCR-I variant (3.10), the value of the objective function indicates the rationalisation factor θ_o by which all inputs can be proportionately decreased without reduction of the outputs. The efficiency scores of both variants are identical due to the intercept theorem of geometry, which is implicitly used in the derivation from (3.4) in Section 3.1.2. Thus, the reciprocal value of the maximum possible productivity increase is equal to the minimum rationalisation factor: $\theta_{\text{CCR-O}} = \theta_{\text{CCR-I}} =: \theta_{\text{CCR}}$ (Thanassoulis et al. 2008, p. 263). However, the specific solutions of both linear programmes for the dominant efficient combination of other DMUs – as the so-called *reference units* or

benchmarking partners – can differ and thus may suggest different benchmarks as
target values, as we will see later on.

The nonnegative linear combinations of the activities $z_j = (x_j; y_j)$ of the
DMUs are used in (3.10) and (3.11) to construct hypothetical points in input/output-
space which can be compared with the observed inputs and outputs of the DMUs.
Nevertheless, one has to bear in mind that these points are purely fictitious for the
time being and only serve for the purpose of performance comparison. In order to
decide which of these points actually represent real production and to qualify them
as potential reference points or benchmarking partners, the performance evaluator
has to consult the specific properties of the transformation process performed by the
DMUs at hand. In the particular case of production based on a linear technology
with constant returns to scale (CRS), all the nonnegative linear combinations of
(3.10) and (3.11) are indeed possible:

$$\mathcal{P} = \left\{ z = \sum_{j=1}^{n} \lambda_j \, z_j \, \middle| \, \lambda \geq 0 \right\} \tag{3.12}$$

The usual **CCR model** in DEA literature is therefore characterised by this precondition. But, if the linearity assumption would lead to invalid combinations, both
optimisation models (3.10) and (3.11) have to be further restricted.

Such restrictions are typically of the form known from (3.9), in which upper and
lower bounds for the activity levels were introduced. The particular case of VRS
with $\tau_{min} = \tau_{max} = 1$ has been proposed by Banker, Charnes and Cooper (1984)
and is called **BCC model**. Hence, the two envelopment forms of either the output-
(**BCC-O**) or the input-oriented variant (**BCC-I**) differ from (3.10) and (3.11) by the
additional restriction: $\sum_{j=1}^{n} \lambda_j = 1$. For **NIRS**, one has the additional restriction:
$0 \leq \sum_{j=1}^{n} \lambda_j \leq 1$, i.e. $\tau_{min} = 0$ and $\tau_{max} = 1$; for **NDRS**: $1 \leq \sum_{j=1}^{n} \lambda_j < \infty$, i.e.
$\tau_{min} = 1$ and $\tau_{max} = 1/\varepsilon$ (with $0 < \varepsilon \ll 1$, i.e. ε is infinitesimally small).

Due to the varying strengths of these restrictions in comparison of the distinct
return to scale properties, the following inequalities generally apply for the (optimal) efficiency scores of the associated linear programmes:

$$\left. \begin{matrix} \theta_{\text{BCC-O}} \geq \theta_{\text{NIRS-O}} \\ \theta_{\text{BCC-I}} \geq \theta_{\text{NIRS-I}} \end{matrix} \right\} \geq \theta_{\text{CCR}} \tag{3.13}$$

$$\left. \begin{matrix} \theta_{\text{BCC-O}} \geq \theta_{\text{NDRS-O}} \\ \theta_{\text{BCC-I}} \geq \theta_{\text{NDRS-I}} \end{matrix} \right\} \geq \theta_{\text{CCR}} \tag{3.14}$$

Therefore, the CCR model is the most rigorous one because it compares the respective DMU with all linear combinations of the other DMUs, and not only with
their convex combinations as is the case with the BCC model.

Important note: If a DMU is *CCR-efficient*, i.e. $\theta_{CCR} = 1$, it is also efficient regarding the other models with NIRS, NDRS or VRS. In particular, any CCR-efficient DMU is *BCC-efficient* in both orientations, too, i.e. $\theta_{BCC-I} = \theta_{BCC-O} = 1$.

The ratios $SE_O = \theta_{CCR}/\theta_{BCC-O}$ and $SE_I = \theta_{CCR}/\theta_{BCC-I}$ are called *scale efficiency* regarding the associated output or input orientation (Banker et al. 1984). Because of (3.13) and (3.14), the following holds:

$$0 \leq SE \leq 1 \tag{3.15}$$

The maximum of 100 % is always attained for CCR-efficient DMUs.

Example 3.4: Six DMUs producing one product y with one factor x

The numerical example is displayed in Figure 3.2. The corresponding data as well as the DEA results are shown in Table 3.1.

The columns 2 and 3 of Table 3.1 contain the corresponding input and output quantities. The ray in Figure 3.2 spanning from the origin through DMUs B and C marks the efficient frontier of the linear envelopment of the six DMUs in the CCR model. Therefore, the four remaining DMUs are CCR-inefficient. Their (in)efficiency scores θ_{CCR} are given in the fourth column of Table 3.1 as percentages, rounded to integer values (as for all such scores in the following tables, too).

Figure 3.2 indicates that DMUs A and D are both BCC-efficient. In this case, different properties are assumed for the underlying technology concerning the data envelopment of the six DMUs, namely convexity, and furthermore often also strong disposability (cf. Sect. 2.4.2 and 3.2.3). Columns 5 and 6 in Table 3.1 contain the input- and output-oriented efficiency scores θ_{BCC-O} and θ_{BCC-I} as well as the scale efficiencies SE_O and SE_I of the six DMUs. Regarding column 5, however, it has to be noted that the scores (of 100 %) of the four BCC efficient DMUs are replaced by their corresponding super-efficiency score (>100 %), e.g. 120 % for DMU B in case of an output-oriented optimisation.

Table 3.1 Data and results of standard DEA models for Example 3.4 (all scores in %)

DMU	x	y	CCR	BCC	SE	$\sum \lambda$
			O&I	O/I	O/I	O/I
A	4	2	50	inf/150	50	67/33
B	6	6	100	120/111	100	100
C	8	8	100	109/113	100	100
D	12	10	83	125/inf	83	150/125
E	10	4	40	44/50	90/80	125/67
F	6	1	17	17/67	100/25	100/17

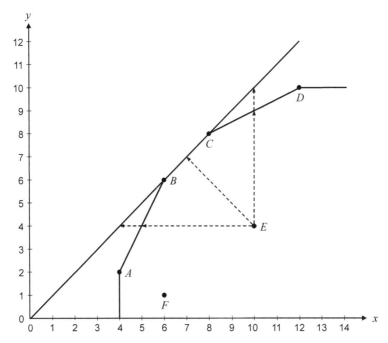

Fig. 3.2 Two-dimensional example with six DMUs (Wojcik et al. 2019, Fig. 1)

The **super-efficiency** score of an efficient DMU can be obtained by excluding the respective DMU from the data envelopment. It takes a value above or equal 100 % and indicates how much an efficient DMU could increase its inputs proportionally, or how much it could decrease its outputs proportionally, without becoming inefficient (Andersen and Petersen 1993). As Figure 3.2 indicates for DMU A in case of BCC-O as well as for DMU D in case of BCC-I, such a super-efficiency score does not always exist. In Table 3.1 (and also in following tables) non-existing super-efficiency scores are marked as 'inf' (= infeasible). Because DMUs B and C lie on the same ray, their CCR super-efficiency scores in column 4 equal 100 %.

The efficient frontier of the NIRS model consists of the line segments spanning from the origin through DMUs B and C up to DMU D. In turn, the efficient frontier of the NDRS model can be described by the line segments from DMU A to B and C and further infinitely along the ray. Therefore, the envelopment of these two models consists of the respective parts of the CCR and the BCC envelopments, which entails similar results for the corresponding models. NIRS and NDRS models are, however, rarely considered explicitly in the literature. Instead, the corresponding return to scale properties of the various DMUs are mostly analysed, given by $\sum_{j=1}^{n} \lambda_j$ from the CCR model variants in column 7 of Table 3.1.

Considering inequalities (3.13) and (3.14) concerning the relationship of the different efficiency scores, one might think at first that up to seven different efficiency scores can occur for a DMU. In that case, the question would arise as to which of the seven scores is the 'right' one. In fact, however, only three distinct efficiency scores are possible for the eight model variants. But, these can differ substantially from each other as Table 3.1 shows. Emrouznejad and De Witte (2010, p. 1580) also remark that there can be "significant differences" between the results of the CCR and BCC model variants. This emphasises the importance of a systematic and justified selection of the return to scale assumption as well as the choice between output or input orientation in any performance analysis based on DEA.

The realisation that for each DMU the eight DEA models attain at most only three different (super) efficiency scores is not a coincidence but rather a regularity. It is based on certain characteristics of Linear Programming. Accordingly, the efficiency score of a NIRS or NDRS model variant must be identical to that of either the CCR model or the BCC model with the same orientation, or of both models if they are equal. That is, in each of the four different inequality chains of (3.13) and (3.14), one of the two inequality signs has to be an equality. In the case of an optimum with $\sum_{j=1}^{n} \lambda_j = 1$, the NIRS and the NDRS efficiency score is identical with the score of the BCC model and, otherwise, that of the CCR model. Nevertheless, it is a priori unpredictable as to which of the two possible scores (CCR or BCC score) for the respective orientation will be attained by a NIRS or NDRS model for the DMU under consideration.

Therefore, column 7 of Table 3.1 displays the sum $\sum_{j=1}^{n} \lambda_j$ of the activity levels for the CCR model variants (3.10) and (3.11) as further information, characterising the respective DEA results of the considered DMU. Since there are two CCR-efficient DMUs on the same ray in Figure 3.2, the value of the sum $\sum_{j=1}^{n} \lambda_j$ depends on the choice of DMU B or C as benchmarking partner; in Table 3.1 the DMU nearest to the reference point is always chosen, i.e. DMU C for DMU D and DMU B for DMUs A and F.

Let us consider the inefficient DMU E for which both DMUs B and C can serve as reference point. Its three efficiency scores in columns 4 and 5 differ only slightly between 40 %, 44 % and 50 % (resulting after rounding from 4/10, 4/9 and 5/10). These scores can readily be derived from the lengths of the four *vertical and horizontal dashed arrows* shown in Figure 3.2. However, as already stressed before, the so-called **reference units** of DMU E on the efficient frontier (shown by the arrowheads in Figure 3.2) as well as the corresponding **benchmarking partners** (DMU C for CCR, respectively DMUs C and D for BCC in the two vertical cases as well as DMU B for CCR, respectively DMUs A and B for BCC in the two horizontal cases) can differ and thus suggest distinct benchmarks as **target values**.

The two scale efficiencies connected with DMU E are vertically $SE_O = 9/10 = 90$ % and horizontally $SE_I = 4/5 = 80$ %. In Figure 3.2, they equal the ratio of the smaller and the larger output or input of the corresponding two reference points onto which DMU E is projected. It must be noted that the actual input or output quantities of DMU E do not play an immediate role in the calculation of the scale efficiency SE. Only the output or input quantities of their two reference points determine the ratio. Thus, scale efficiencies describe the distance between the BCC and the CCR efficient frontiers regarding those parts of the frontier onto which the considered DMU is projected subject to the chosen orientation. For example, the scale efficiency of DMU E is 100 % (instead of 90 % or 80 %) if it is not projected vertically or horizontally, but simultaneously in both directions onto the line segment between DMUs B and C, as shown by the third, *bisecting dashed arrow* to the upper left.[7] As another example, DMU F leads to $SE_O = 6/6 = 100$ %, but $SE_I = 1/4 = 25$ %.

Important note: It makes no sense to talk of the scale efficiency of a single DMU *without disclosing its supposed projection onto the efficient frontier*. In fact, scale efficiency is a property which characterises the distance of the CCR and the BCC efficient frontier, and in no way, it is a property of any inefficient DMU itself.[8]

The same crucial reservation has to be made regarding the returns to scale of a DMU. In production theory, they are originally defined solely as a property of the whole technology (Dyckhoff and Spengler 2010, p. 63). This can be generalised as a *local property* – for the neighbourhood *of certain parts of the efficient frontier* – that characterises the extent of the total trade-off between inputs and outputs (Cooper et al. 2007, Chap. 5). If it is proportional, we have CRS, otherwise variable, in particular increasing (IRS) or decreasing (DRS) returns to scale if the outputs change progressively or degressively with the inputs.

Hence, in Figure 3.2 we have IRS along the line segment between DMUs A and B, CRS between B and C as well as DRS between C and D. In this sense, the efficient frontier of the BCC model in the neighborhood of the respective reference point of DMU E shows DRS if E is projected vertically $\left(\sum \lambda_j = 125\ \% > 100\ \%\right)$, IRS if projected horizontally $\left(\sum \lambda_j = 67\ \% < 100\ \%\right)$ as well as CRS if projected to the upper left by the bisecting arrow $\left(\sum \lambda_j = 100\ \%\right)$. However, returns to scale are not defined (or infinite) for DMU E itself, because, for any (strongly) inefficient point, it is even possible to increase (all) outputs without increasing any input or to decrease (all) inputs without decreasing any output.

---

[7] E.g. by an unoriented additive model with equal weights for the input and output slacks (as will be further discussed in the next subsection).

[8] In this sense, Dyckhoff et al. (2009) have used scale efficiencies to empirically characterise the returns to scale of the best practice research production function of German business schools.

3.2.2   Unoriented Additive Performance Measurement

In Example 3.4, the significant difference in the BCC-efficiency scores of DMU F between 17 % and 67 % (precisely: 1/6 and 2/3) originates from the fact that F is projected onto a *weakly efficient* part of the data envelopment in case of an input orientation. That is why the linear programmes (3.10) and (3.11) – eventually including a further constraint regarding the returns to scale – are usually complemented by an infinitesimally small summand in their objective function or by a second optimisation step, which identifies possible slacks for individual inputs and outputs. In this way, the originally purely radial projections of inefficient DMUs are modified, so that (strongly) efficient points of the envelopment will be identified as benchmarks and targets, e.g. data point A for DMU F in the case of an input orientation. However, the radial efficiency score itself remains the same, so that it only indicates weak efficiency in general.

To avoid this deficit of weak efficiency inherent to all radial DEA models, *(slack-based) additive models* can be used instead. These models take all *slacks* s_i^- and s_r^+ in the definition of the efficiency measure into account. Such a slack represents the *individual improvement* of the respective type of input (= cost) or output (= benefit). Thus, they directly identify strongly efficient solutions, without the additional calculations which are necessary for radial models. Because of its compatibility with the radial models, the model introduced by Tone (2001) is particularly suitable for enabling comparisons to the results of the standard DEA models. Moreover, since it is often hardly possible to justify the orientation of a model meaningfully in DEA applications, the absent orientation of slack-based models represents yet another advantage. Instead of (3.10) and (3.11), the unoriented *Tone-model* takes the following nonlinear form:

$$\text{Minimise} \quad \rho_0 = \frac{1 - \dfrac{1}{m}\left(\displaystyle\sum_{i=1}^{m} \frac{s_i^-}{x_{i0}}\right)}{1 + \dfrac{1}{s}\left(\displaystyle\sum_{r=1}^{s} \frac{s_r^+}{y_{r0}}\right)}$$

$$\text{such that} \quad \sum_{j=1}^{n} \lambda_j \cdot x_{ij} + s_i^- = x_{io} \quad \text{for } i = 1, \dots, m$$

(3.16)

$$\sum_{j=1}^{n} \lambda_j \cdot y_{rj} - s_r^+ = y_{ro} \quad \text{for } r = 1, \dots, s$$

$$\lambda_j,\ s_i^-,\ s_r^+ \geq 0 \quad \text{for } i = 1, \dots, m;\ j = 1, \dots, n;\ r = 1, \dots, s$$

To facilitate the calculation, model (3.16) can be *linearised* (Tone 2001; Cooper et al. 2007, Chap. 4.4.3). Additionally, a super-efficiency score can be determined (Tone 2002). However, because its definition differs from that one of the efficiency score, the super-efficiency score cannot be easily compared with that of the radial models.

Model (3.16) supposes CRS. If we add – analogously to (3.10) or (3.11) – further constraints in an appropriate form for (3.16), we obtain corresponding versions of the Tone-model with VRS, NIRS or NDRS. With the same reasons as for (3.13) and (3.14), the following applies:

$$\theta_{\text{Tone,VRS}} \geq \begin{Bmatrix} \theta_{\text{Tone,NIRS}} \\ \theta_{\text{Tone,NDRS}} \end{Bmatrix} \geq \theta_{\text{Tone,CRS}} \qquad (3.17)$$

Furthermore, also in the case of slack-based models, its NIRS and NDRS versions must each attain one of the efficiency scores under CRS and VRS so that each DMU can have a maximum of two distinct efficiency scores due to absence of input or output orientation.

For his efficiency scores, Tone (2001, p. 502) proved an important property, which, besides the appropriate definition, is essentially based on the consideration of all slacks:

$$\theta_{\text{Tone,CRS}} \leq \theta_{\text{CCR}} \qquad (3.18)$$

An analysis of his proof given for the CCR-I model shows that it is equally valid when the set of feasible solutions for linear programme (3.16) is further restricted by a constraint regarding the returns to scale. Accordingly, inequality (3.18) is applicable to all (input-oriented standard radial) models with other forms of returns to scale. The same proposition can be proved in a similar way for the output-oriented models. The respective radial efficiency score tallies exactly with that of the Tone-model if the DMU considered is strongly efficient. In that case, no slacks occur, so that efficiency scores under the respective returns to scale are both 100 %. Therefore, in cases of inefficient DMUs, the Tone-efficiency score generally attains a value which is genuinely smaller than the corresponding radial efficiency score. Thus, an advantage of the Tone-model is its much better discrimination between the inefficient DMUs, so that the differences between them are elucidated more clearly (Wojcik et al. 2019).

Example 3.5 (3.4 continued): Six DMUs producing one product with one factor
For the purpose of illustration, Table 3.2 contains the results of the Tone-model for the six DMUs of Example 3.4 shown in Figure 3.2. Because of non-comparability of the super-efficiency scores, columns 4 and 5 display the usual score 100 % in case of (here always strong) efficiency.

In case of CRS the efficiency scores of the Tone-model (column 4) are identical to those of the radial (CCR) model (column 4 of Table 3.1), also in case of VRS (columns 5) necessarily for the efficient DMUs, but not for the inefficient ones where they are smaller (as stated in general before). Since their VRS score equals its CRS score, the scale efficiencies of both inefficient DMUs E and F are 100 %, i.e. they are projected to the line between DMUs B and C with CRS in Figure 3.2. For DMUs A to D, the SE scores equal those of the radial models. In the particular case of our numerical example, all those points on the ray (as efficient frontier for CRS) build reference points which dominate the respective DMU under consideration. Benchmarking partners are the DMUs B or C.

Table 3.2: Results of the Tone-model variants for Example 3.4 (all scores in %)

DMU	x	y	CRS	VRS	SE	$\Sigma \lambda$
A	4	2	50	100	50	33
B	6	6	100	100	100	100
C	8	8	100	100	100	100
D	12	10	83	100	83	150
E	10	4	40	40	100	100
F	6	1	17	17	100	100

3.2.3 Essentiality of Disposability Assumptions

When determining the right DEA model for performance evaluation, often also disposability assumptions are considered. In addition to the potential conflict with reality and environmental objectives (discussed in Sect. 2.4.1), Dyckhoff and Allen (2001, p. 319) have stated a further reason against generic technological disposability axioms, namely that they are often not necessary in order to determine the (in)efficiency of production activities. This can easily be demonstrated by a slight modification of the (slacks-based) *additive DEA model* with fixed weights w^b and w^c for the output and input slacks (indicating benefit and cost improvements), here for CRS as example (with weights e.g. chosen such as in the linearised Tone-model):

Maximise $\quad w^b \cdot s^b + w^c \cdot s^c$

such that $\quad \displaystyle\sum_{j=1}^{n} \lambda_j x_j \leq x = x_0 - s^c$

$$\sum_{j=1}^{n} \lambda_j y_j \geq y = y_0 + s^b \tag{3.19}$$

$$s^b, s^c \geq 0; \ \lambda \geq 0$$

Strong (or *free*) *disposability* is expressed in this linear programme by two additional inequalities for attainable inputs x and outputs y. Without this further assumption, these two inequalities have to be fulfilled with equality. In any case, however, the inequalities themselves are redundant. In no circumstance will they ever influence the strongly efficient points of the production frontier of the data envelopment. That is, both linear programmes, with and without these inequalities, have identical optimal solutions, independent of the enlargement of the PPS by the allowed disposal of outputs or augmentation of inputs.

Dakpo et al. (2016) have accepted this to a certain extent. Concluding their review with "challenges and future trends of research", they remark (p. 357):

> In fact, the 'no-disposability' assumption advocated by Dyckhoff and Allen (2001) can be accounted for by measuring a Pareto-Koopmans efficiency (non-radial) measure where all the slacks are considered given the preference structure of the technology. Our last recommendation is thus related to how this 'no-disposability' assumption can be modelled and how it can be associated to the preference structure in the DEA framework.

Nevertheless, radial DEA models do not need a disposability assumption either. This can easily be understood already by inspecting the two-dimensional example of Figure 3.2. Here we will demonstrate it graphically by a simple three-dimensional numerical example of the BCC-I model.

Example 3.6: Three DMUs producing one output with two inputs

The three DMUs $j \in \{A, B, C\}$ all produce one unit of an output ($y_{1j} = 1$) with different amounts (x_{1j}, x_{2j}) of two factors, e.g. labour and energy. The three observed factor combinations are $(5; 5)$ for A, $(12; 3)$ for B, and $(10; 14)$ for C. Figure 3.3 displays both input possibility sets. Without free factor disposability the triangle built by the DMUs forms the PPS; with disposability the area above and to the right of the dotted lines starting in points A and B is additional part of the PPS. The *bold line segment* joining A and B describes the identical *efficient frontier* for both cases. Obviously, DMU C is inefficient with an efficiency score of 50 % and with DMU A as (strongly efficient) benchmarking partner.

Usually, as the first step in DEA with free disposal, DMU C is radially projected along the *dashed line on the ray down to point* C_1 as a target point with the same factor mix within the enlarged input possibilities nearest to the origin. Since C_1 is weakly efficient only, its factor combination $(5; 7)$ can be improved in a second step of DEA by eliminating a 'slack' of two input units of the second factor energy. This, however, implies a different factor mix, i.e. new proportions of factor combination, namely that DMU C has to become more labour- than energy-intensive.

Nevertheless, there is a second possible path (shown by the other two dashed arrows in Figure 3.3) for projecting DMU C onto its benchmarking partner A. This path is fully contained in the convex hull of the three DMUs (shaded triangle) and thus does not make use of any disposability assumption. It is achieved by exchanging the two steps of traditional DEA. Here, DMU C first reduces slack by changing its factor mix to the proportions on that *ray from the origin through the points of the efficient frontier* nearest to it. In our example, the second factor is to be reduced by four input units, thus determining the factor combination $(10; 10)$ as intermediate (target) point C_2 with an efficient factor mix. The second step projects C_2 radially onto A as usual, thereby reducing both inputs by 50 % again.

The efficiency calculation is not at all affected by assumptions of strong or free disposability. The main reason for this fact is that such an assumption modifies the PPS (by enlarging it) but does not affect its efficient frontier itself, and hence also not the solution of the DEA model (Joro and Korhonen 2015, p. 30). This is analogously true for the extended strong disposability axiom in case of undesirable products and factors (which will be considered in the next section) as well as for the assumption A8 of disposability of benefits and costs (introduced in Sect. 2.3.2) regarding the value efficient frontier of the VPS in the general case of MCPT.[9]

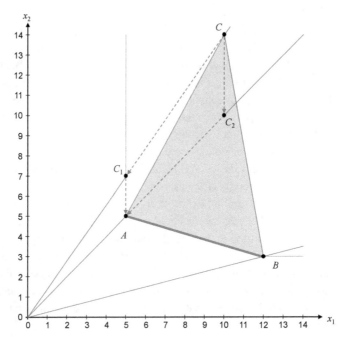

Fig. 3.3 Irrelevance of strong disposability for the efficient frontier of a convex PPS (Dyckhoff 2019, Fig. 3)

---

[9] In contrast, the other disposability assumptions developed in the literature (and reviewed by Dakpo et al. 2016) do change the efficient frontier in general. Therefore, they must have a convincing technological justification. It is namely to be questioned why the envelopment of the measured activities of the observed DMUs does not already contain all technologically possible (disposal) activities, particularly in cases of disposal technologies, such as e.g. waste incineration plants (Wojcik et al. 2017).

3.3 DEA for the Standard Case of Goods and Bads

Now, linear value functions of another very special type are supposed that nevertheless generalise the one before by the existence of bads besides the goods. They have been defined in Section 2.2.1:

A6b (Trade-off of goods and bads): Different types of non-financial costs are measured by each input of a good and each output of a bad, i.e. $c = (x^G; y^B)$; and, vice versa, each output of a good as well as each input of a bad defines one type of the benefits, i.e. $b = (x^B; y^G)$.

As already mentioned, this is a standard assumption for environmentally oriented performance evaluation, characterised by the existence of undesirable (by-)products and factors. By 2015, there were more than 350 academic DEA papers studying undesirable products, but only 22 papers on undesirable factors (Wojcik et al. 2017). In an overview, Zhou and Liu (2015) formulated various DEA models with "undesirable inputs and outputs", without referring to any systematic approach as to how they can possibly be deduced in general. However, if one applies the approach of generalising DEA by MCPT (introduced in Sect. 3.1), such models are immediately derived.

Let us demonstrate this for the additive DEA model (3.19) as an example, but without any disposability assumption. Its corresponding *multi-criteria (slack-based weighted) additive DEA model* for a PPS $\mathcal{P}$ defined by (3.9) is:

Maximise $\quad w^c \cdot s^c + w^b \cdot s^b$

such that $\quad c(z) + s^c = c(z_0)$

$$b(z) - s^b = b(z_0) \tag{3.20}$$

$$s^c, s^b \geq 0; z \in \mathcal{P}$$

With assumption A6b, we obtain the following (slack-based weighted) *additive DEA model for goods* (G) *and bads* (B) as inputs (I) as well as outputs (O):[10]

Maximise $\quad w^{GI} \cdot s^{GI} + w^{BO} \cdot s^{BO} + w^{GO} \cdot s^{GO} + w^{BI} \cdot s^{BI}$

such that $\quad \displaystyle\sum_{j=1}^{n} \lambda_j x_j^G + s^{GI} = x_o^G$

$$\sum_{j=1}^{n} \lambda_j y_j^B + s^{BO} = y_o^B \tag{3.21}$$

---

[10] Zhou and Liu (2015, p. 422) have formulated the same model without any reasoning. If the objective function of linear programme (3.20) is substituted by the analogously generalised efficiency measure (3.16) of Tone (2001), the corresponding DEA model formulated by Zhou and Liu (2015, p. 423) results (Wojcik et al. 2017, p. 480).

$$\sum_{j=1}^{n} \lambda_j \boldsymbol{y}_j^{G} - \boldsymbol{s}^{GO} = \boldsymbol{y}_o^{G}$$

$$\sum_{j=1}^{n} \lambda_j \boldsymbol{x}_j^{B} - \boldsymbol{s}^{BI} = \boldsymbol{x}_o^{B}$$

$$\boldsymbol{s}^{GI}, \boldsymbol{s}^{BO}, \boldsymbol{s}^{GO}, \boldsymbol{s}^{BI} \geq \boldsymbol{0}; \ \lambda = (\lambda_1, \dots, \lambda_n) \in S$$

Here, bad output is mathematically described in the same way as good input, and bad input like good output. With respect to MCPT as underlying theory presented in Chapter 2, it should be clear, however, that this identity is only of a syntactic and not at all of a semantic nature. The two must not be confused! In the approach by MCPT, the primary variables of efficiency analysis are benefits and costs, not inputs and outputs: "Considering pollutants as inputs is not a correct way of modelling pollution-generating technologies"[11]. Indeed, pollutants are outputs, however of a kind which implies (social) costs.

In the special case (3.21) of model (3.20), the benefits are measured by the physical quantities of good outputs and bad inputs, the costs by those of good inputs and bad outputs (as a kind of proxy variables). Consequences of a production activity that one wishes to reduce are always costs, be it for the input of goods (because of expenditures for buying them) or for the output of bads (because of their damage to nature or of emission fees to be paid). Consequences to be maximised are the benefits, in (3.21) either resulting from the output of goods (usually because of the revenues for selling them) or from the input of bads (because one must get rid of them, as in the example of tyres incinerated by a cement plant).[12] In any case, it should be borne in mind that the preferences for objects as either goods or bads have *a priori* nothing to do with the production technology. In (3.20) and (3.21), the actual production possibilities are in fact modelled as usual in traditional DEA, namely by a linear or convex envelopment of the DMUs independently of the preferences for inputs and outputs.

Remark: Model (3.21) is the first published DEA model with *undesirable factors* (Dyckhoff and Allen 2001, p. 315). Zhou and Liu (2015, p. 422) have formulated the same model, in spite of a different, technologically motivated definition of those factors. Their notion of 'undesirable input' is in contrast to the preference-based view of MCPT, which in turn, however, is consistent with their own definition of *desirable outputs* as "what the decision maker hopes to produce as much as possible", reflecting a subjective judgment by Zhou and Liu (2015, p. 417). On the other hand, they state (p. 417) "that the desirability of inputs should be defined according to the intrinsic production mechanism. (...) If the increase of an input will not increase the desirable outputs, then it

---

[11] Dakpo et al. (2016, p. 357), while misinterpreting Dyckhoff and Allen (2001).

[12] Nevertheless, the valuation of old products, like scrap tyres or used paper on markets, may be mixed or changing, sometimes valued as 'good' with a positive price, sometimes as 'bad' with a negative price, depending on the actual decision situation at hand, particularly on supply and demand (Dyckhoff 1992, pp. 6 and 69). This is a crucial problem for products that cannot be stored, e.g. in power generation with renewables when there is too much wind or sun (Fandel and Lorth 2009, p. 416).

is classified as undesirable" (and vice versa for 'desirable input'). However, the increase of a *limitational*, i.e. non-substitutable production factor alone, e.g. (new) tyres in car assembly, without increasing other factors at the same time, will neither increase nor decrease the output of the main product (car). Hence, according to the definition of Zhou and Liu, limitational factors would have to be classified as inputs which are simultaneously both desirable as well as undesirable. Furthermore, waste incineration plants do not have material desirable outputs (unless simultaneously producing power or heat as a marketable by-product) so that their input 'waste' cannot be classified in this technological way of Zhou and Liu.

Nevertheless, if the service of disposal is understood as an output of waste incineration plants, then waste input can be classified as desirable by the technologically motivated definition of Zhou and Liu (2015). This coincides with Dyckhoff and Allen (2001, p. 315), who introduced the preference-based notion of *desired input* into DEA: "Waste to be burned at the power plant is such an undesirable object the destruction of which is desired, i.e. the input of which should be maximized."

The inconsistent use of the term '(un)desirable input' in the literature leads to a terminological confusion, not only in DEA but also in economics. Its cause may also be the ambiguity of the terms 'input' and 'output', depending on whether they represent a *flow* of objects going into or coming out of a process, or whether they denote the objects themselves, as a *stock* of things. Bads are undesired things. Hence, not only a stock of bads is undesired, but also their output, because it increases the stock. In contrast, the *input of bads*, e.g. waste such as scrap tyres in the context of cement production, is *desired* while reducing their undesired stock. This classification of inputs and outputs into desired and undesired ones is independent of the technological connection between inputs and outputs determined by the transformation process and depends solely on the preferences of the decision maker or evaluator (Dyckhoff 1992, p. 65; Wojcik et al. 2017).

Surveys of DEA literature show that measuring environmental performance is one of the main strands of recent development (Liu et al. 2013a,b; Lampe and Hilgers 2015). Consequently, special surveys of this strand try to give some overview of the knowledge developed so far (e.g. Song et al. 2012; Zhang and Choi 2014; Dakpo et al. 2016). In their review of bads as inputs, Wojcik et al. (2017) find it striking that all radial DEA models with data transformation for the input or output quantities of bads must assume VRS in order to avoid distortions of the efficiency evaluation of the DMUs. Such data transformations typically multiply the quantities of bads by −1 and add the same large enough constant to all those quantities in order to achieve positive numbers. Then, the assumption of VRS is purely mathematically motivated and does not need to conform with the actual properties of the real production possibilities underlying the transformation processes of the considered DMUs. Data transformations in empirical sciences have to be justified by arguments of measurement theory with respect to the application area at hand. To neglect this important requirement is a serious deficit of all DEA models applying the core idea of data transformation to measure the performance of DMUs without respective reflections, particularly in cases with the input or output of bads.

In order to show that such data transformations are unnecessary we use as further example the cost-oriented CCR model (3.6) for a PPS $\mathcal{P}$ defined in (3.9) with CRS:

Minimise $\qquad \theta_o$

such that $\qquad c(z) \le \theta_o c(z_o)$ and $b(z) \ge b(z_o)$

$$\text{for } z = \sum_{j=1}^{n} \lambda_j z_j \text{ with } \lambda_j \ge 0,\, j = 1,\dots,\, n \qquad (3.22)$$

Inserting the benefits and costs of the standard case A6b leads to the following radial DEA model with bads as input and output (first stated by Wojcik et al. 2017, p. 481):

Minimise $\qquad \theta_o$

such that $\qquad \displaystyle\sum_{j=1}^{n} \lambda_j x_{ij}^{\mathrm{GI}} \le \theta_o x_0^{\mathrm{GI}} \qquad\qquad\qquad\quad \text{for } i \in \mathrm{GI}$

$$\sum_{j=1}^{n} \lambda_j y_{rj}^{\mathrm{BO}} \le \theta_o y_0^{\mathrm{BO}} \qquad\qquad\qquad \text{for } r \in \mathrm{BO}$$

$$\sum_{j=1}^{n} \lambda_j x_{ij}^{\mathrm{BI}} \ge x_0^{\mathrm{BI}} \qquad\qquad\qquad\quad \text{for } i \in \mathrm{BI} \qquad (3.23)$$

$$\sum_{j=1}^{n} \lambda_j y_{rj}^{\mathrm{GO}} \ge y_0^{\mathrm{GO}} \qquad\qquad\qquad\quad \text{for } r \in \mathrm{GO}$$

$$\lambda_j \ge 0 \qquad\qquad\qquad\qquad\qquad\quad \text{for } j = 1,\dots,n$$

3.4 DEA for General Linear Value Functions

Finally, we consider general linear cost and benefit functions according to property A6c of Section 2.2.2:

$$c_\kappa(x,y) = \sum_{i=1}^{m} c_{\kappa,i} \cdot x_i + \sum_{r=1}^{s} c_{\kappa,m+r} \cdot y_r \quad \text{for } \kappa = 1,\dots,k$$

$$b_\beta(x,y) = \sum_{i=1}^{m} b_{\beta,i} \cdot x_i + \sum_{r=1}^{s} b_{\beta,m+r} \cdot y_r \quad \text{for } \beta = 1,\dots,\ell \qquad (3.24)$$

Dyckhoff and Ahn (2010) have used such functions to derive linear programmes for the ***multi-criteria CCR model with linear value functions***, namely the linear ***multiplier form*** of the cost-oriented DEA model according to (3.5):

$$\Theta_o^* = \max B_o = \sum_{i=1}^{m} \tilde{\mu}_i x_{io} + \sum_{r=1}^{s} \tilde{\mu}_{m+r} y_{ro}$$

$$\text{such that } \sum_{i=1}^{m} \tilde{v}_i x_{io} + \sum_{r=1}^{s} \tilde{v}_{m+r} y_{ro} = 1 \qquad (3.25)$$

$$\sum_{i=1}^{m}(\tilde{\mu}_i - \tilde{v}_i)x_{ij} + \sum_{r=1}^{s}(\tilde{\mu}_{m+r} - \tilde{v}_{m+r})y_{rj} \leq 0 \qquad \text{for } j = 1,\dots,n$$

$$\tilde{v}_\rho = \sum_{\kappa=1}^{k} v_\kappa c_{\kappa\rho}; \qquad \tilde{\mu}_\rho = \sum_{\beta=1}^{\ell} \mu_\beta b_{\beta\rho} \qquad \text{for } \rho = 1,\dots,m+s$$

$$v_\kappa \geq 0, \mu_\beta \geq 0 \qquad \text{for } \kappa = 1,\dots,k; \ \beta = 1,\dots,\ell$$

as well as according to (3.6) and (3.22) the following *envelopment form*:

$$\theta_o^* = \min \theta_o$$

such that $$\sum_{i=1}^{m} b_{\beta,i}(x_i - x_{io}) + \sum_{r=1}^{s} b_{\beta,m+r}(y_r - y_{ro}) \geq 0 \qquad \text{for } \beta = 1,\dots,\ell$$

$$\sum_{i=1}^{m} c_{\kappa,i}(x_i - \theta_o x_{io}) + \sum_{r=1}^{s} c_{\kappa,m+r}(y_r - \theta_o y_{ro}) \leq 0 \qquad \text{for } \kappa = 1,\dots,k$$

$$x_i = \sum_{j=1}^{n} \lambda_j x_{ij} \qquad \text{for } i = 1,\dots,m \qquad (3.26)$$

$$y_r = \sum_{j=1}^{n} \lambda_j y_{rj} \qquad \text{for } r = 1,\dots,s$$

$$\lambda_j \geq 0 \qquad \text{for } j = 1,\dots,n$$

The relationship between these two models and the original input-oriented CCR-models (as the simplest special case, i.e. with $c = x$ and $b = y$) is no longer immediately obvious. For the envelopment form, the restrictions of the benefit types $\beta = 1,\dots,\ell$ and the cost types $\kappa = 1,\dots,k$ comprise the generalisation from the input- to the cost-oriented model by means of MCPT. For the multiplier form, it is above all the new multiplier variables $\tilde{v}_\rho$ and $\tilde{\mu}_\rho$ for the inputs and outputs that are derived from the multipliers for the cost and benefit types.[13]

Remark: In general, the number of input and output types $(m + s)$ does not correspond to the number of cost and benefit types $(k + \ell)$. In principle, it can be both more or less. This can again be illustrated by applications to environmental protection. For example, chlorofluorocarbons (CFC), on the one hand, were banned largely from production and consumption world-wide under the 1987 Montreal Protocol because of their harmful effect on atmospheric ozone ('ozone hole' above the Antarctic). In an eco-efficiency analysis, the output y_{CFC} would have to be recorded as costs in the corresponding environmental impact category (*ozone depletion potential*): $c_{ODP} = y_{CFC}$. On the other hand, the group of fluorocarbons (HFCs) also contributes to the greenhouse effect, along with other known greenhouse gases such as carbon dioxide (CO_2), methane (CH_4) and nitrous oxide (N_2O). The CFC output must therefore be considered separately as ecological costs for two different environmental impact categories. Conversely, the negative climate effects of the emissions of various greenhouse gases can be aggregated by means of so-called carbon dioxide equivalents with regard to their effect on climate change in their overall effect (*global warming potential*):

---

[13] Dyckhoff and Ahn (2010, pp. 1266ff.) show applications of model (3.26) for a modified version of Example 3.7.

$$c_{GWP} = y_{CO2} + 28y_{CH4} + 265y_{N2O} + 8500y_{CFC} + \cdots \qquad (3.27)$$

This means that one mass unit of methane has about 28 times more greenhouse potential (GWP over 100 years) than one mass unit of carbon dioxide and that the other greenhouse gases have even much more (cf. Myhre et al. 2013, p. 731 and the illustrative Example 2.1 in Sect. 2.1.2). While the corresponding greenhouse effect of the gases is well documented from a scientific point of view and while their emissions can generally be measured relatively easily, the further effects caused by their immissions into the atmosphere are difficult to assess in terms of their impacts on the ecosystem Earth as well as on the human society, especially if it should be evaluated in monetary terms (cf. Fig. 3.4 in Sect. 3.5).

With respect to their eco-efficiency measurement method by means of DEA, Kuosmanen and Kortelainen (2005, p. 69) suggest: "If possible, it is useful to first aggregate specific emissions and pollutants using impact assessment tools." We will prove an appropriate proposition in the following which states non-improving performance ratings of each DMU in cases of consistent, monotonically nested, multistage linear value functions. Before doing that, this essential property will first be demonstrated by a modified version of Example 2.1 of Section 2.1.2.

Example 3.7 (2.1 continued): Hierarchy of linear valuations

Different from the data of Figure 2.2, no social impacts are taken into account for the performance analysis of the four cement factories, and, apart from purely economic objectives, only global warming is considered as an ecological cost. Instead of CFC we include methane (CH_4) as second emission besides carbon dioxide. These modifications eliminate potentially conflicting impacts of the same input or output (in particular labour as input simultaneously reflecting economic and social interests), otherwise violating the consistency property A6e of Section 2.3.3.

Hierarchy Level 1

$$
\begin{bmatrix}
4 & 4 & 5 & 3 \\
3 & 5 & 5 & 5 \\
120 & 40 & 100 & 100 \\
6 & 2 & 5 & 5 \\
1 & 1 & 1 & 1 \\
5 & 1 & 3 & 3
\end{bmatrix}
\begin{bmatrix}
c_1 \\ c_2 \\ c_3 \\ c_4 \\ b_1 \\ b_2
\end{bmatrix}
\overset{\Delta}{=}
\begin{bmatrix}
x_1 \\ x_2 \\ y_2 \\ y_3 \\ y_1 \\ x_3
\end{bmatrix}
=
\begin{array}{l}
\text{labour} \\
\text{capital} \\
CO_2 \\
CH_4 \\
\text{cement} \\
\text{scrap tyres}
\end{array}
$$

$$
\begin{array}{cccc}
100 & 100 & 80 & 100 \\
\end{array}
\quad \theta
$$

At the lowest level of the linear value aggregation hierarchy, we analyse the technical efficiency in line with the standard assumption A6b of goods and bads in environmental DEA (cf. Sect. 2.2.1 and 3.3). The respective value impact matrix V (cf. Sect. 2.2.2 and Theorem 3.1) considers the six types of technological inputs and outputs of the example as immediate decision consequences to be directly maximised or minimised. Thus, as shown above, labour and capital input

represent two distinctive kinds of economic costs to be minimised[14] (not necessarily measured in the same units), together with CO_2 and CH_4 emissions as two
further kinds of non-financial costs, here ecological ones. The quantity of cement
produced, and the quantity of scrap tyres safely disposed of, are the two kinds of
benefits each to be maximised (in its natural units). The cost-oriented CCR
model (3.23) then calculates efficiency scores of 100 % for all DMUs except the
third one with a score of 80 %. Thus, DMU C is technically inefficient.

Hierarchy Level 2

$$
\begin{bmatrix} 288 & 96 & 240 & 240 \\ 190 & 290 & 300 & 280 \\ 440 & 360 & 400 & 400 \end{bmatrix} \triangleq \begin{bmatrix} \bar{c}_1 \\ \bar{c}_2 \\ \bar{b}_1 \end{bmatrix} = \begin{bmatrix} c_3 + 28c_4 \\ 10c_1 + 50c_2 \\ 340b_1 + 20b_2 \end{bmatrix} \quad \begin{matrix} \text{greenhouse effect} \\ \text{financal cost} \\ \text{revenue} \end{matrix}
$$

$$
\begin{matrix} 100 & 100 & 80 & 83 & \theta \end{matrix}
$$

At the second level of the hierarchy, the six attributes of level 1 are aggregated
– consistently with the prior preferences – into three types of values being more
fundamental to the decision maker or evaluator. Accordingly, the undesirable
outputs CO_2 and CH_4 are combined in terms of their greenhouse effect, resulting
in a single kind of ecological costs usually measured in units of radiative forcing
(or carbon dioxide equivalents), where one mass unit of methane will have the
same impact as 28 units of carbon dioxide within 100 years. A second kind of
costs is obtained by adding the financial values of workers' salaries and capital
expenses. These costs are specified separately from the financial benefit through
the revenues from cement sales and scrap tyre disposal. Now, the fourth DMU
D is also found to be (value) inefficient (D: 83 % and C: 80 %).

Hierarchy Level 3

$$
\begin{bmatrix} 288 & 96 & 240 & 240 \\ 250 & 70 & 100 & 120 \end{bmatrix} \triangleq \begin{bmatrix} \hat{c}_1 \\ \hat{b}_1 \end{bmatrix} = \begin{bmatrix} \bar{c}_1 \\ \bar{b}_1 - \bar{c}_2 \end{bmatrix} \quad \begin{matrix} \text{greenhouse effect} \\ \text{profit} \end{matrix}
$$

$$
\begin{matrix} 100 & 84 & 48 & 58 & \theta \end{matrix}
$$

The next step is to subtract financial costs from financial revenues, as is usually done in monetary accounting to calculate profit. Thus, on the third level,
greenhouse effect and financial profit are the only two remaining performance
criteria. Since none of the four DMUs makes losses, the cost-oriented CCR
model (3.22) can be applied once again. Now, only DMU A is 100 % (value)
efficient. The other scores are 84 % for B, 48 % for C and 58 % for D.

The example shows how linear value functions allow for systematic multi-stage
nested performance evaluations in the form of a hierarchy. If the aggregation is

---

[14] As the only difference between DMUs C and D is the amount of labour input, DMU D (weakly)
dominates DMU C.

preferentially consistent, the performance results of a DMU are monotonically decreasing. An aggregation is (**preferentially**) **consistent** when benefits on the lower level are linearly combined with nonnegative coefficients into benefits and with nonpositive ones into costs on the higher level, and the analogous holds true for the costs (cf. Sect. 2.3.3). Thus, regarding DEA, Theorem 2.4 and Corollaries 2.5 and 2.6 can be continued as follows.

Theorem 3.2: If a multi-criteria DEA model for a DMU is consistently aggregated by linear value functions into a DEA model of the same type on a higher hierarchy level, then the efficiency scores of the DMUs cannot improve.

Proof: Since the DEA models in envelopment form of both hierarchy levels are of the same type of linear programme, also their dual linear programmes in multiplier form are of the same type. By inserting the linear value functions into the dual linear programme of the higher level, one obtains exactly the dual linear programme of the lower level; however, with the additional constraints that the multipliers of two aggregated costs or benefits have to be proportional to the respective two coefficients of the linear value function. Hence, the optimal efficiency score of this restricted dual linear programme representing the higher level cannot be better than that of the original dual linear programme of the lower level.

The performance rating of a DMU can only decline when the evaluation is aggregated – or at best remain constant – as long as the preference relations expressed by the corresponding value functions of the hierarchy are consistent. Example 3.7 has demonstrated this essential property of hierarchical performance evaluations for a 3-level hierarchy.

Corollary 3.3: Under the assumptions of Theorem 3.2, performance scores at lower levels of aggregation constitute an upper bound for performance scores at higher levels.

3.5 Further Insights and Conclusions

As with carbon dioxide and methane in (3.27) and in Example 3.7, *life cycle assessment* (LCA) methods usually aggregate ecological impacts by linear value functions hierarchically (cf. Fig. 1.2). If this is done with fixed weights, one must be careful not to violate rationality conditions such as the *independence from irrelevant alternatives* (Dyckhoff et al. 2015; cf. Sect. 4.3). DEA, as generalised by MCPT in this chapter (*MC-DEA*), supplies a less demanding evaluation method for aggregating the ecological impacts than the correct application of MAUT. As Kuosmanen and Kortelainen (2005, p. 65) note: "The DEA eco-efficiency score provides an upper bound for the 'true' but unknown eco-efficiency index: using any other weights will necessarily decrease the eco-efficiency score of the evaluated unit".

Theorem 3.2 delivers a further important argument supporting the use of DEA in practice. That is, the technological inputs and outputs of a DMU are often more easily observable and measurable than the state of the fundamental goals, which are actually the ultimate focus of interest (Kuosmanen and Kortelainen 2005, p. 61). Although it is true that performance criteria should ideally represent fundamental values as much as possible, in practice they often represent means to an end only. As we have seen in Example 3.7, MC-DEA nevertheless allows for meaningful estimations of the performance of a DMU as long as inputs and outputs as well as benefits and costs are chosen compatibly with the fundamental objectives.

On the one hand, the more the benefits and costs represent the fundamental goals, the better (i.e. sharper) the performance ratings. On the other hand, the relationship between the inputs and outputs of a transformation process at the one end and the fundamental sustainability goals at the other is often complex and it is difficult to untangle the chain of effects (Kuosmanen and Kortelainen 2005, p. 61). Consider, for example, the network of impacts of greenhouse gas emissions with respect to global warming on human welfare and the ecosystem. As shown in Figure 3.4, most parts of the full chain of effects – from the outputs via several connected implied outcomes to the last fundamental values – are outside the sphere of influence of the respective DMU and its available production technology. It is a challenge to take account of such complex impact chains when applying DEA for ecological performance evaluations, particularly in the case of nonlinearities (cf. Sect. 2.3.1).

Nevertheless, the essential advantage of MC-DEA in comparison to traditional DEA is that it allows the user to strictly differentiate technological from non-technological assumptions, i.e. those concerning the actual (inputs and outputs of the considered) transformation process from those of value impact aspects. Hence, it forms a further step to a broader conceptual framework for "measuring eco-efficiency of production with DEA" (Kuosmanen and Kortelainen 2005 and already Dyckhoff and Allen 2001 afore). By evaluating pressures instead of emissions,

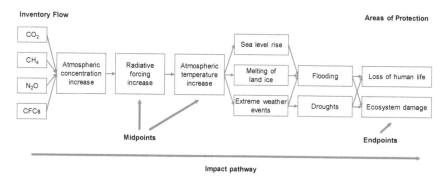

Fig. 3.4 From outputs via impacts to fundamental goals (cf. Hauschild and Huijbregts 2015, Fig. 1.2)

Kuosmanen and Kortelainen (2005, p. 70) understand their paper "as a step toward integrating the perspective of environmental impact assessment in industrial ecology with the frontier approach of environmental performance management in economics into a unified framework".

There are areas other than sustainability management and ecological economics where a non-financial performance evaluation generalised by MCPT can play an important role in research and practice, too, even in fields of classical business administration, such as management accounting, production control and logistics. Example 3.7, calculating profit as a benefit at the last stage of (value impact) aggregation, has shown that such a generalised performance evaluation can also be understood as a kind of management accounting for uncertain or unknown prices. After more than forty years of development, DEA has not been very successful in those classical areas of business administration until now, despite the fact that performance measurement is one of the most prevalent topics in business administration practice.

MC-DEA, however, allows for a clear discrimination between the possible production activities under the full control of a DMU (the PPS) on the one hand, and their consequences for markets and other economic, social or ecological environments, modelled by multiple value functions, on the other hand. In the DEA literature, though, there are many examples of applications that take financial parameters as inputs or outputs without reflecting on the reality of the underlying assumptions, such as convexity or even linearity, that are being made. This ignores the fact that the results of such an DEA investigation depend strongly on the performance criteria as well as the particular DEA model chosen (Wojcik et al. 2019). Thus, MC-DEA throws a better light on some of the open questions in DEA "prior to choosing a model" (Cook et al. 2014) as well as in respect of interpreting the results of efficiency analyses obtained with such models.

Nevertheless, this chapter – in particular Theorem 3.1 – has also shown, that the mathematics of MC-DEA is identical with that of traditional DEA if the value functions are linear (and hopefully preferentially consistent). Then, DEA models can be applied in the same formal way as usual, namely in that the benefits and costs are handled as if they were 'outputs' and 'inputs', respectively. It is exactly this what is meant by the second part of the statement by Cook et al. (2014), which we have cited and criticised at the beginning of Section 3.1.1. It is a standard procedure that takes place in a lot of DEA applications in the literature, usually without any reflection on the underlying assumption on the chosen 'inputs' and 'outputs' regarding their dependency on the real production inputs and outputs. Indeed, if the underlying value functions are linear and are inserted for the benefit and cost variables, one obtains specific new DEA models for the original input and output variables, as shown in this chapter. Some of the models derived in this way are well known, especially from the DEA literature on undesirable outputs.

References

Afsharian M, Ahn H, Neumann L (2016) Generalized DEA – An approach for supporting input/output factor determination in DEA. Benchmarking: An International Journal 23:1892–1909

Andersen P, Petersen NC (1993) A procedure for ranking efficient units in Data Envelopment Analysis. Management Science 39:1261–1264

Banker RD, Charnes A, Cooper WW (1984) Some models for estimating technical and scale inefficiencies in Data Envelopment Analysis. Management Science 30:1078–1092

Barr RS (2004) DEA software tools and technology – A state-of-the-art survey. In: Cooper WW, Seiford LM, Zhu J (ed): Handbook on Data Envelopment Analysis. Springer, Boston et al., pp 539–566

Belton V (1992) Integrating data envelopment analysis with multiple criteria decision analysis. In: Goicoechea A, Duckstein L, Zionts S (ed): Proc. IXth Internat. Conf. Multiple Criteria Decision Making. Springer, Berlin, pp 71–79

Charnes A, Cooper WW, Rhodes E (1978) Measuring efficiency of decision making units. European Journal of Operational Research 2:429–444

Charnes A, Cooper WW, Golany B, Seiford L (1985) Foundations of data envelopment analysis for Pareto-Koopmans efficient empirical production functions. Journal of Econometrics 30:91–107

Coelli TJ, Prasada Rao DS, O'Donnell CJ, Battese GE (2005) An Introduction to Efficiency and Productivity Analysis. 2nd ed, Springer, New York

Cook WD, Tone K, Zhu J (2014) Data envelopment analysis: Prior to choosing a model. Omega 44:1–4

Cooper WW, Seiford LM, Tone K (2007) Data Envelopment Analysis – A Comprehensive Text with Models, Applications, References and DEA-Solver Software. 2nd ed, Springer, New York

Dakpo KH, Jeanneaux P, Latruffe L (2016) Modelling pollution-generating technologies in performance benchmarking: Recent developments, limits and future prospects in the nonparametric framework. European Journal of Operational Research 250:347–359

Demski JS, Feltham GA (1976) Cost Determination: A Conceptual Approach. Iowa State University Press, Ames

Doyle RH, Green JR (1993) Data envelopment analysis and multiple criteria decision making. Omega 21:713–715

Dyckhoff H (1992) Betriebliche Produktion: Theoretische Grundlagen einer umweltorientierten Produktionswirtschaft. Springer, Berlin et al.

Dyckhoff H (2018) Multi-criteria production theory: Foundation of non-financial and sustainability performance evaluation. Journal of Business Economics 88:851–882 (DOI 10.1007/s11573-017-0885-1; open access)

Dyckhoff H (2019) Multi-criteria production theory: Convexity propositions and reasonable axioms. Journal of Business Economics 89:719–735

Dyckhoff H, Ahn H (2010) Verallgemeinerte DEA-Modelle zur Performanceanalyse. Zeitschrift für Betriebswirtschaft 80:1249–1276

Dyckhoff H, Allen K (2001) Measuring ecological efficiency with Data Envelopment Analysis (DEA). European Journal of Operational Research 132:312–325

Dyckhoff H, Spengler T (2010) Produktionswirtschaft. 3rd ed, Springer, Berlin et al.

Dyckhoff H, Rassenhövel S, Sandfort K (2009) Empirische Produktionsfunktion betriebswirtschaftlicher Forschung: Eine Analyse der Daten des Centrums für Hochschulentwicklung. Zeitschrift für betriebswirtschaftliche Forschung 61:22–56

Dyckhoff H, Quandel A, Waletzke K (2015) Rationality of eco-efficiency methods: Is the BASF analysis dependent on irrelevant alternatives? International Journal of Life Cycle Assessment 20:1557–1567

Dyson RG, Allen R, Camanho AS, Podinovski VV, Sarrico CC, Shale EA (2001) Pitfalls and protocols in DEA. European Journal of Operational Research 132:245–259

Emrouznejad A, De Witte K (2010) COOPER-framework: A unified process for non-parametric projects. European Journal of Operational Research 207:1573–1586

Fandel G, Lorth M (2009) On the technical (in)efficiency of a profit maximum. International Journal of Production Economics 121: 409–426

Färe R, Grosskopf S, Lovell CAK (1994) Production frontiers. Cambridge University Press, Cambridge

Frisch R (1965) Theory of Production. D Reidel Publ, Dordrecht

Halme M, Joro T, Korhonen P, Salo S, Wallenius J (1999) A value efficiency approach to incorporating preference information in data envelopment analysis. Management Science 45:103–115

Hauschild MZ, Huijbregts MAJ (2015) Life Cycle Impact Assessment. Springer, Dordrecht

Joro T, Korhonen P (2015) Extension of Data Envelopment Analysis with Preference Information. Springer, New York

Joro T, Korhonen P, Wallenius J (1998) Structural comparison of data envelopment analysis and multiple objective linear programming. Management Science 44:962–970

Kuosmanen T, Kortelainen M (2005) Measuring eco-efficiency of production with Data Envelopment Analysis. Journal of Industrial Ecology 9:59–72

Lampe HW, Hilgers D (2015) Trajectories of efficiency measurement: A bibliometric analysis of DEA and SFA. European Journal of Operational Research 240:1–21

Liu JS, Lu LYY, Lu WM, Lin BJY (2013a) Data envelopment analysis 1978-2010: A citation-based literature survey. Omega 41:3–15

Liu JS, Lu LYY, Lu WM, Lin BJY (2013b) A survey of DEA applications. Omega 41:893–902

Myhre G, Shindell D, Bréon F-M, Collins W, Fuglestvedt J, Huang J, Koch D, Lamarque J-F, Lee D, Mendoza B, Nakajima T, Robock A, Stephens G, Takemura T, Zhang H (2013): Anthropogenic and Natural Radiative Forcing. In: Change Stocker, TF, Qin D, Plattner G-K, Tignor M, Allen SK, Boschung J, Nauels A, Xia Y, Bex V, Midgley PM (eds.): Climate Change 2013: The Physical Science Basis. Contribution of Working Group I to the Fifth Assessment Report of the Intergovernmental Panel on Climate. Cambridge University Press, Cambridge/New York, pp 659–740

Song M, An Q, Zhang W, Wang Z, Wu J (2012) Environmental efficiency evaluation based on data envelopment analysis: A review. Renewable and Sustainable Energy Reviews 16:4465–4469

Thanassoulis E, Portela MCS, Despic O (2008) Data Envelopment Analysis: The mathematical programming approach to efficiency analysis. In: Fried HO, Knox Lovell CA, Schmidt SS (ed) The Measurement of Productive Efficiency and Productivity Growth. Oxford University, New York, pp 251–420

Tone KA (2001) A slacks-based measure of efficiency in data envelopment analysis. European Journal of Operational Research 130:498–509

Tone KA (2002) A slacks-based measure of super-efficiency in Data Envelopment Analysis. European Journal of Operational Research 143:32–34

Wallenius J, Dyer JS, Fishburn PC, Steuer RE, Zionts S, Deb K (2008) Multiple Criteria Decision Making, Multiattribute Utility Theory: Recent Accomplishments and What Lies Ahead. Management Science 54:1336–1349

Wojcik V (2018) Performanceanalyse mittels Verallgemeinerter Data Envelopment Analysis: Vorgehensmodell und Evaluation. Dr. Kovač, Hamburg

Wojcik V, Dyckhoff H, Gutgesell S (2017) The desirable input of undesirable factors in Data Envelopment Analysis. Annals of Operations Research 259:461–484

Wojcik V, Dyckhoff H, Clermont M (2019) Is data envelopment analysis a suitable tool for performance measurement and benchmarking in non-production contexts? Business Research 12(2): 559–595 (DOI 10.1007/s40685-018-0077-z; open access)

Zhang N, Choi Y (2014) A note on evolution of directional distance function and its development in energy and environment studies 1997–2013. Renewable and Sustainable Energy Reviews 33:50–59

Zhou Z, Liu W (2015) DEA models with undesirable inputs, intermediates, and outputs. In: Zhu J (ed): Data Envelopment Analysis. Springer, New York, pp 415–446

Zhu J (ed) (2015) Data Envelopment Analysis. Springer, New York

Chapter 4
Challenges of Performance Evaluation in Practice[1]

Abstract. The previous two main chapters of this brief book describe a funda-mental theory and an important methodology of non-financial performance evalua-tion. Traditional production theories and data envelopment models are generalised in such a way that key performance indicators are represented by multiple, a priori incommensurable cost and benefit functions which are defined on inputs and out-puts of the activities to be evaluated. This last chapter sketches selected further as-pects and challenges that are essential for performance evaluation in practice. In particular, it is concerned with (1) balance and specialisation as performance cate-gories in addition to effectiveness and efficiency; (2) the identification, selection and qualitative differentiation of the inputs and outputs that determine the consid-ered costs and benefits; (3) the influence of the choice of compared activities and of exogenous weighting factors on the relative performance; (4) approaches to detect dependencies of the performance indicators from the inputs and outputs, even though they are often not quantifiable; and (5) more comprehensive concepts and systems of performance management and management accounting which may in-clude the topics covered in this book.

Keywords   Balance versus specialisation • Balanced scorecard • Independence of irrelevant alternatives • Key performance indicator • Performance management • Qualitative dominance

---

[1] Section 4.3 is adapted from Dyckhoff, Quandel and Waletzke (2015b) by permission of Springer Nature.

4.1 Balance and Specialisation as Performance Categories

The measurement of effectiveness and efficiency forms the core of performance evaluations in general. As already stated in Section 1.1, there may be further categories of rationality that are relevant in particular cases, e.g. legitimacy or sustainability. This section addresses an approach of Dyckhoff et al. (2015a), integrated within data envelopment analysis (DEA), that determines the *balance* and the *specialisation* of a decision-making unit's (DMU) activity with respect to the multiple kinds of costs and benefits as key performance indicators. Usually, individuals or organisations as DMUs can choose to concentrate on a sample of ends, only, putting aside the others. For instance, one university can prioritise research, whereas another one focuses on teaching. Therewith, certain profiles of specialisation can be expressed with respect to some given standard of **balanced** ends. Thus, a DMU can be called **specialised** if its relation of ends differs from a given balanced relation.

Until now, the method of DEA-integrated balance or specialisation measurement has been developed for output-oriented radial DEA models only, where the outputs represent the main ends (Dyckhoff and Gutgesell 2015). It calculates a specific kind of deviation of the output quantities from predetermined balanced relations.

Example 4.1: Five balanced and four specialised DMUs

As illustrative example, Figure 4.1 presents the output-diagram of nine DMUs $A, \dots, I$ which produce two types of outputs y_1 and y_2 with identical quantities $x_1 = 1$ of one input. It also shows the convex data envelopment of these DMUs, displaying strongly disposable outputs, resulting from the usual assumptions of the literature regarding a BCC model (cf. Sect. 3.2.1 and 3.2.3). Table 4.1 contains the data (columns 2 to 4) as well as the relevant results. Because of the identical input quantity of all DMUs, the CCR-O and BCC-O efficiency scores θ (column 5) are not only identical, but also measure the *effectiveness* of the DMUs regarding both outputs as main ends.

The *shaded subset* $\mathcal{B}$ inside the data envelope marks the intersection of it with a pointed cone starting from the origin. It is assumed that this cone represents all combinations of both outputs which are considered as a 'entirely balanced' output mix (in view of exogenously given information), defined by a maximal **balance score** of $\beta = 100\,\%$ or a minimal **specialisation degree** of $\sigma := 1 - \beta = 0\,\%$. All points of the data envelope outside this cone feature a balance score between 0 % and 100 %, namely DMUs A, B, H and I. The balance score of a point outside $\mathcal{B}$, e.g. DMU A or H, can be determined by projecting this point appropriately, e.g. by reducing only that output which is produced relatively too much considering the DMU's balance. The corresponding points inside $\mathcal{B}$, here A' and H', have a lower efficiency score (that can simply be determined by the line ratios $\overline{0A'}/\overline{0A''}$ and $\overline{0H'}/\overline{0H''}$ respectively). The balance is then determined by the ratio of the two points' efficiency scores (A vs. A', H vs. H'): $\beta := \theta_b/\theta$. The scores for balanced efficiency θ_b and balance β in the example are given by columns 6 and 7 of Table 4.1. Points belonging to $\mathcal{B}$ are projected onto themselves, thus fulfilling the condition $\beta = 100\,\%$.

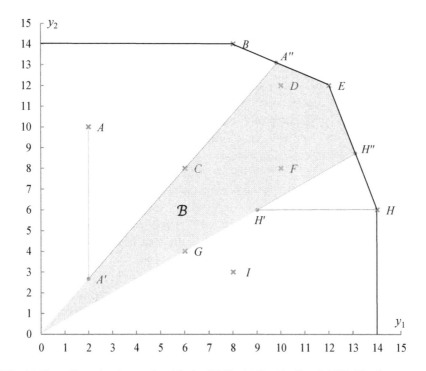

Fig. 4.1 Three-dimensional example with nine DMUs (cf. Dyckhoff et al. 2013, Fig. 1)

Table 4.1 Balance measurement for a 3-dimensional example with nine DMUs (all scores rounded in %; cf. Dyckhoff et al. 2013, Table 1)

DMU	x_1	y_1	y_2	θ	θ_b	β
A	1	2	10	71	20	29
B	1	8	14	100	81	81
C	1	6	8	61	61	100
D	1	10	12	94	94	100
E	1	12	12	100	100	100
F	1	10	8	79	79	100
G	1	6	4	46	46	100
H	1	14	6	100	69	69
I	1	8	3	57	34	60

The approach of Dyckhoff et al. (2015a) deliberately places high requirements on the balance score. That is achieved by two conditions: $(x_o; y_b)$ is dominated by $(x_o; y_o)$ and has the highest possible efficiency score. These conditions result in a nonlinear optimisation model, which is not easily to be solved in general (Dyckhoff and Gutgesell 2015). There are two exceptions: first, the case of only two outputs, as in the example of Figure 4.1, where the problem can be solved graphically; second, the case of more than two outputs with an extremely reduced balance cone which is identical to a ray, i.e. the output ratios of balanced output mixes are fixed. The approach can be transferred from output-oriented radial DEA models to non-oriented additive slack-based models (Sect. 3.2.2) if one accepts that the efficient target point itself is not necessarily balanced.

There are three applications of this approach in case studies with real data until now. They are concerned with the research performance of 55 German business schools (Dyckhoff et al. 2013), the economic efficiency of 20 pharmacy stores (Dyckhoff et al. 2015a) and the welfare of 27 countries of the European Union (Wojcik et al. 2019). Regarding the first mentioned case study, Figure 4.2 displays the effectiveness and the complementary balance scores for the business schools (BS) with respect to the data of the Centre of Higher Education (CHE) where 100 % research balance is defined by the relations of the median values of the three considered performance indicators. In the 2-dimensional diagram, the *five most reputed business schools* are marked by ×, the *next eight reputed* by +, the *remaining 42* by •. The quite irregular dispersion of all 55 points (with a gap between the best performing BS and the other, shown by the dotted lines) illustrates the weak correlation between effectiveness on the one hand and specialisation on the other hand regarding the performance indicators chosen by CHE as research 'output'. Nevertheless, it can be seen from the diagram that the five most reputed business schools are at least 90 % effective as well as four (two) of them are more than 70 % (90 %) balanced.

The performance indicators used by the CHE are publications (in points), PhD-dissertations (number) and expended third-party funds (in €) gained over a three-year period. Here, third-party funds are actually an *input* into the ongoing research process. However, Sections 2.2.2 and 3.4 have shown that they may be used technically as an 'output' in standard DEA models – indicating the *benefit* of a greater opportunity of future research findings – if they depend linearly on the actual inputs and outputs of the research activities. Furthermore, the production possibility set has to be convex or linear in reality in line with the underlying assumptions of the applied DEA model (as a 'must' in all DEA applications).

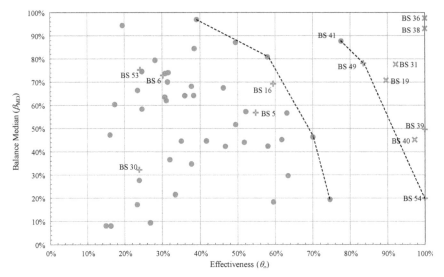

Fig. 4.2 Research effectiveness and balance of 55 German business schools (Dyckhoff et al. 2013, Fig. 3)

4.2 Selection and Qualitative Differentiation of Inputs and Outputs

Section 3.1.3 has explained why Theorem 3.1 forms the main proposition of multi-criteria production theory (MCPT) for applications to DEA. It states for linear value functions that the image of a convex (or linear) envelopment of activities in input/output-space equals the convex (respectively linear) envelopment of the image points of these activities in cost/benefit-space. Therefore, neither the explicit knowledge of the relevant inputs and outputs nor that of the respective linear value functions are necessary in order to determine the (value) efficiency scores of the DMUs. Hence, if the premises of Theorem 3.1 are true in an actual instance, it suffices to know solely the values of the relevant costs and benefits of the DMUs. Thus, Theorem 3.1 supplies a factual justification of the usual mathematical DEA models if they are applied to the costs and benefits instead of to the inputs and outputs. Otherwise, however, one has to determine the relevant types of inputs and outputs as well as their influence on the considered costs and benefits.

Concerning the determination of the actual input and output types – in DEA literature often called 'factors'[2] – three main kinds of problems have been addressed in the DEA literature:

- *Selection of object types* (e.g. Wagner and Shimshak 2007): Which input types and output types are relevant in a certain context, which are not?
- *Dual-role types* (e.g. Cook and Zhu 2007): Should certain object types (e.g. bank deposits or third-party funds) be characterised as input or as output?
- *Undesirable objects* (e.g. Seiford and Zhu 2002): How should undesirable input objects (e.g. waste incinerated in a power plant) and undesirable output objects (e.g. emissions of such a plant) be taken into account?

The last problem is answered in Section 3.3 (Wojcik et al. 2017). The second one has to face the fundamental difference between the technological categories of input and output on the one hand and the value categories of cost and benefit on the other (cf. Ahn and Lee 2014; 2016 for a first attempt regarding bank efficiency). Chapter 2 has revealed this categorial distinction by presenting MCPT. As far as the first problem is concerned, we have pointed out already in Section 1.2.1 that there is a countless number of things, which takes part of a production process or influence it. Belton and Stewart (1999, p. 91) state that "it is impossible to escape value judgements in the building of a DEA model; the selection of inputs and outputs is in itself inherently subjective". Disregarding the need for subjective choices in DEA is a major source of problems in applications, causing doubts on their validity in reality.

However, taking notice of MCPT as one of DEA's scientific foundations makes it possible to unlock all of the knowledge and know-how of decision theory, together with specific findings of production research. Because such extensions would go far beyond the scope of this book, we refer to the general well-known literature of decision making and performance management regarding the specification of objectives and performance criteria. Moreover, we think that – except generic frameworks – such attempts should better be specific for the respective application domain (Afsharian et al. 2016).

This section addresses a different topic, connected with the specification of relevant input and output types. It allows to expand the concepts of dominance and efficiency, considered so far, with respect to qualitative valuations. For this purpose, a more subtle distinction is made regarding the objects being input or output of a production (or consumption) activity. An object *type* is thus further differentiated into various *sorts* of this type representing distinct qualities which can be compared, at least ordinally. Objects of the same sort are considered identical with respect to the performance evaluation. Objects of different sorts of the same type can often be

---

[2] Because '(production) factor' usually denotes an input and not an output (in economics and elsewhere), we use the term 'type' instead.

distinguished into higher or lower quality while (input or output) objects of different types cannot be compared in this sense.

Souren (1996a) developed an approach to distinguish between different object sorts even in a quantitative manner. This is achieved by explicitly modelling their ingredients or *components*. Often, the total quantity of an input i $(i = 1, ..., m)$ can be specified by the subquantities of relevant components, while the same holds for the quantity of the outputs r $(r = 1, ..., s)$. Since component quantities may be zero, each relevant input or output object type is determined by a certain constellation of one and the same set of components f $(f = 1, ..., F)$ without loss of generality. For the sake of simplicity, the following analysis assumes a mass balance of components, so that each object quantity can be totally split up in its components' quantities:

$$x_i = \sum_{f=1}^{F} x_{if}$$

$$y_r = \sum_{f=1}^{F} y_{rf}$$

(4.1)

The quotients $q_{if} = x_{if}/x_i$ and $q_{rf} = y_{rf}/y_r$ determine the *relative content* of component f within an object, usually specified as percentages, summing up to 100 %. A *sort* of input or output objects of type t is defined by a specific constellation of component contents. An object *type* t is determined by its associated sorts, i.e. by the allowed constellations of component contents which are considered as different from each other and represent varying qualities of this type (Souren 1996a, Sect. 6.2.1).

Example 4.2: Waste sorting processes

In order to illustrate this component concept, Figure 4.3 shows four different processes of sorting packaging waste. The sole, identical input in each alternative process is a *waste mix* (WM) in quantity 1,200 kg that consists of 500 kg (41.67 %) aluminium (f = AL), 500 kg (41.67 %) paper&pulp (f = PP) and 200 kg (16.67 %) of miscellaneous materials (f = MM). Sorting results in three different output object types, namely two *secondary raw materials* (SRM-AL and SRM-PP) mostly consisting of either aluminium or paper&pulp (at least 90 %), and a *residual waste* (RW) that – for reasons of simplicity – consists of miscellaneous materials only. The four alternative sorting processes differ with respect to the resulting quantities of the three output object types (SRM-AL, SRM-PP, RW) as well as their particular constellations of the three component quantities (AL, PP, MM).

Comparing the four alternatives, decision makers may realise that, on the one hand, a pure comparison of the object types' quantities (SRM-AL, SRM-PP, RW) leads to a wrong valuation because qualitative differences are not considered appropriately. If, on the other hand, each output sort would be classified as usual as a distinct, incomparable object type, the alternatives cannot be compared at all – because every alternative would then contain different object types. This dilemma may be solved by a closer look on the components' contribution to object sorts' description as well as performance valuation. Hence, an assumption how the component quantities and object qualities are valued is needed (which further differentiates those of category A6 in Chapter 2). Three examples are presented in the following.

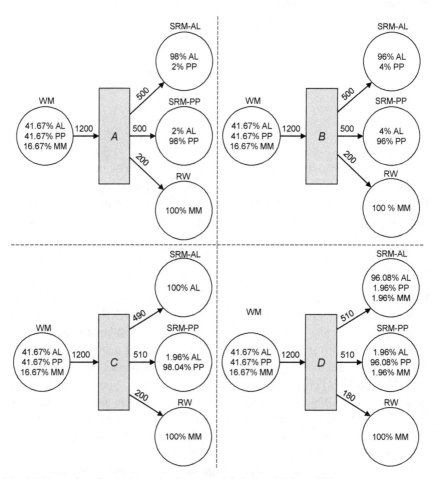

Fig. 4.3 Alternatives for sorting packaging waste (cf. Souren 1996a, p. 109)

Example 4.3 (4.2 continued): Pure valuation of correctly sorted component quantities
Let us first consider a waste manager who wants to evaluate the four different sorting alternatives described in Figure 4.3 solely by comparing the staff's accurateness when separating the aluminium and paper&pulp fractions into the right secondary raw material containers. Therefore, only the aluminium fraction in SRM-AL and the paper&pulp fraction in SRM-PP are considered to have a positive impact (benefit) on the value of the appropriate SRM object types, namely AL on SRM-AL and PP on SRM-PP. All other fractions, in particular the misthrows of PP or MM into SRM-AL and of AL or MM into SRM-PP, have a negative one (cost[3]); the quantity of residual waste can be neglected.

Then, process C dominates A because $(490 \cdot 1.00 =)$ 490 kg AL and $(510 \cdot 0.9804 =)$ 500 kg PP are sorted correctly with C versus 490 kg AL and 490 kg PP with A while 10 kg AL are placed incorrectly with both processes and 10 kg PP additionally with A. A dominates both B and D because the other two processes do not sort more of AL and PP correctly into the SRM object types while moreover exhibiting more misthrows. Thus, alternative C is the only efficient one. It contains the highest quantities of aluminium in SRM-AL (490 kg) and paper&pulp in SRM-PP (500 kg) and the least incorrectly placed quantities, i.e. paper in SRM-AL (none), aluminium in SRM-PP (10 kg) and miscellaneous materials in both secondary raw materials (none).

The example illustrates one of more possibilities to expand the concept of value dominance and value efficiency (introduced in Sect. 2.1.3) by including component quantities – either as a complement or even as a substitution of object quantities.

Example 4.4 (4.2 and 4.3 continued): Technical performance indicators
Another waste manager considers two technical sorting performance indicators often used in practice as appropriate measures: *separation degree* and *purity*. They also emphasise the relevance of the accurate separation of the target fractions. The separation degree serves as a yield measure of effectiveness and is defined by the quotient of the material fraction quantity sorted into the right SRM container divided by the material included in the packaging waste input. Purity serves as a quality measure and is defined by the share of the correctly sorted material fraction in the suitable SRM, thus equal to the corresponding relative component content. Table 4.2 shows the values for the two separation degrees and purities for all alternatives.

The different values can be interpreted as four kinds of benefits of the sorting process. Comparing them leads to the following conclusions almost identical as

---

[3] Other often relevant costs of sorting processes are labour expenses for the sorting done by workers or their time effort. For reasons of simplicity theses costs are neglected when comparing the four alternatives.

before: Process C dominates all three other processes, while A dominates B and D. Different from Example 4.3, B is now dominated by D, too. This slight difference results from the fact that misthrows are no longer valued as separate costs.

Table 4.2 Separation degrees and purities of the sorting alternatives [in %]

	Activity A	Activity B	Activity C	Activity D
Separation degree Aluminium	98	96	98	98
Purity Aluminium	98	96	100	96.08
Separation degree Paper&Pulp	98	96	100	98
Purity Paper&Pulp	98	96	98.04	96.08

Both Examples 4.3 and 4.4 show possible specifications of performance measurements where absolute or relative component quantities serve as benefits and costs. Nevertheless, an exclusive consideration of component quantities to specify object quality disregarding object quantities can lead to wrong decisions (Souren 1996b, p. 15).

Example 4.5 (4.2 – 4.4 continued): Quantitative valuation with quality restrictions
A third waste manager evaluates the four alternatives with respect to their sales opportunity at the SRM market. The customers on this market buy SRM only with a purity higher than 95 %. As SRM can be further processed irrespective of its exact quality – as long as the purity-threshold is not undercut – it is now classified as one and the same object sort with an identical value. The profits then only depend on the SRM quantities as relevant benefits. Since all alternatives meet the quality restriction (cf. the purity values in Table 4.2), sorting process D (with 510 kg of SRM-AL and SRM-PP each) is the only efficient one. Processes A, B and C do not dominate each other; A and B are even equivalent concerning the benefits.

The Examples 4.2 – 4.5 reveal that object quality can play a vital role in performance measurement. Which benefits and costs are appropriate – and sufficient – indicators for the comparison of alternatives depends on the preferences relevant for the intended evaluation. The consideration of quality aspects, by component specification or in any other form, allows for a more distinct performance evaluation. Hence, one is no longer forced into the dilemma to clearly separate between different object types, but has the opportunity to include quality aspects, either as sole or supplementary benefits and costs or at least as restrictions when classifying object sorts.

An open question of further research is how to combine the above sketched component concept with the data envelopment methodology analysed in Chapter 3. This will surely prove to be practically fruitful since the technology of sorting processes seems to be linear or at least convex (and therefore one main prerequisite for the application of DEA is fulfilled).

4.3   Choice of Alternatives and Weighting Factors

The main advantage of the data envelopment methodology is that the (in realistic situations often small) set of considered activities can be substantially extended by comparable, synthesised new ones. Whether the prerequisites of DEA application – in particular the linearity or convexity of the PPS at least in the relevant domain – are fulfilled is a question regularly not given enough attention to in the DEA literature (Wojcik et al. 2019). But, without a valid knowledge of the features of the underlying PPS, the set of activities cannot easily be amended by further admissible ones which would allow for a better comparison by dominance considerations typical in DEA. Then, however, a more distinct performance evaluation for a defined set of alternatives needs more information about those characteristics which may be relevant for the evaluation – e.g. such as the qualitive ones explained in the last section.

Instead of enlarging the set of comparable alternatives, the standard approach is to reduce the set of performance criteria. As we have seen in Section 3.4 regarding (generalised) DEA, the more the criteria represent the fundamental goals, the better (i.e. sharper) the performance rating. Usually this is achieved by looking for convincing arguments which allow to aggregate at least some of the multiple distinct cost and benefit types into fewer ones – although the former have been incommensurable, *a priori*. As is well-known from economic contexts, typical arguments lead to trade-off relations between different types of criteria derived from market prices or other observed human behaviour. As we have illustrated already in Section 1.2 regarding ecological and social evaluations, aggregation in these contexts, e.g. in life cycle assessment (LCA), also tries to use such trade-off relations. They may be gained from objective scientific facts, such as e.g. the radiative forcing effects of different greenhouse gases within a defined time horizon, or from social preferences, which in turn may be derived from legal norms or also from actual human behaviour.

Trade-offs between different performance criteria yield weights for these criteria. One must, however, be careful with the definition and use of such weights because their numerical values strongly depend on the circumstances of derivation as well as on the numerical scales used (Eisenführ et al. 2010, Sect. 6.6 – 6.7). Otherwise, rationality principles may be violated. One such principle requires the *independence from irrelevant alternatives*, i.e. the choice between two alternatives should not be influenced by the existence or non-existence of a third alternative (Eisenführ et al. 2010, p. 7).

Dyckhoff et al. (2015b) have demonstrated a violation of this principle by the well-known method of *eco-efficiency analysis* (EEA) of BASF which is based on standard practice for life cycle assessment (LCA). It is a method for the relative evaluation of the economic and ecological performance of products or processes, developed in 1996 by the chemical firm together with management consultants and introduced into the scientific literature by Saling et al. (2002). Since then, more than 600 application studies have been conducted globally on behalf of the business and customers of BASF (Saling 2016).

EEA aggregates ecological impacts by linear value functions hierarchically in three steps according to Figure 1.3. They partially employ fixed factors for social preferences and are subject of the so-called *range effect* in determining the weights for the ecological impacts.[4]

Example 4.6: Influence of an irrelevant alternative (data adapted from Kleine et al. 2004)

The example is based on a BASF study on alternatives for the disposal of soil contaminated by petroleum-derived hydrocarbon (Kleine et al. 2004). The study aimed at the decision, whether ground preparation or dumping of the contaminated soil was preferable under consideration of ecological and economic criteria. Table 4.3 shows the data for just three of the six alternatives in the aforementioned study, all of them representing ground preparation methods: Alternatives A and B correspond to the microbiological processes of type 1 (MB1) and type 3 (MB3), and alternative C corresponds to the washing process (W). To be able to illustrate the violation of the rationality principle by the EEA method, compared with the original data for alternative A, the energy value was increased by 3,000 MJ and the cost value decreased by 205 €. Both modifications result in values below or between those of the alternatives B and C, i.e. the data for alternative A is still realistic.

EEA is now applied first to the two alternatives A and B in *sample 1*, only, and afterwards to all three alternatives A, B and C in *sample 2*. In any case, the principle of independence from irrelevant alternatives demands that the inclusion of alternative C in sample 2 should not influence the preference order of the alternatives A and B in comparison to sample 1 when applying the EEA (or any other decision support tool). Alternative C is not dominated by either of the other two alternatives. Nevertheless, it seems to be the worst of all three alternatives and therefore appears to be totally irrelevant. When compared with alternative B, it shows a slightly better value just for energy (28,576 MJ versus 30,029 MJ) and apart from that, worse values, e.g. significantly for emissions to water, despite higher cost; compared with alternative A, it has better values only for POCP and resource consumption.

---

[4] Although EEA has evolved over the years since 1996 to meet changing methodological, market and customer needs, these shortcomings seem to exist also in more recent versions of the method, as far as their incomplete description suggests (Uhlman and Saling 2017).

Table 4.3 Basic data for the disposal of contaminated soil (cf. Dyckhoff et al. 2015b, Table 1)

Alternatives / Criteria	A	B	C
Global warming potential (GWP) [CO_2 equivalents]	2 551 615	2 958 240	3 804 116
Ozone depletion potential (ODP) [CFC equivalents]	0.0005	0.0001	0.0126
Photochemical ozone creation potential (POCP) [ethene equivalents]	1 849	1 505	1 537
Acidification potential (AP) [SO_2 equivalents]	17 037	18 583	19 986
Emissions to water [crit. vol. cbm]	12 235	8 039	227 417
Emissions to soil [weighted mass]	4 223	4 241	5 280
Energy impacts [MJ]	25 752	30 029	28 576
Resource consumption [weighted kg]	11 247	9 524	11 002
Land use [weighted sqm]	12	12	12
Toxicity potential – production [evaluation points]	550	350	1 250
Toxicity potential – utilisation [evaluation points]	3 500	2 800	17 700
Toxicity potential – deposit/disposal [evaluation points]	50	50	50
Risk potential – pollution by traffic [evaluation points]	1.0	1.0	1.0
Risk potential – uncertainty of decline [evaluation points]	0.5	1.0	2.0
Risk potential – burden of change to the status quo [evaluation points]	0.0	0.0	2.5
Costs [€]	3 119	3 116	3 331

Table 4.4 shows the violation of the rationality axiom occurring when applying EEA on both samples. The last row displays the total ecological impact where a smaller value is preferred to a higher one. While alternative B is ecologically preferable over A in sample 1 (0.953 > 0.950), the preference order changes in favour of alternative A (0.689 < 0.693) when including alternative C (0.993). In a reverse perspective, the preference order $A \succ B$ changes into $A \prec B$ when alternative C is eliminated from sample 2.

Besides the total ecological impact, Table 4.4 displays the weighted normalised values of each of the six ecological impact categories of the second to last ecological aggregation level of EEA, already shown in Figure 1.2. The analysis of the according preferences for the alternatives A and B demonstrates that in all ecological impact categories the preferences between A and B are identical for sample 1 and sample 2. However, the preference order changes in the final aggregation stage. Thus, the violation of the rationality axiom takes place immediately when calculating the total ecological impact.

Table 4.4 Weighted, normalised ecological impacts of EEA (cf. Dyckhoff et al. 2015b, Table 2)

Alternatives \\ Criteria	Sample 1 (S1)			Sample 2 (S2)				S2/S1 [%]	
	A	B	Most polluting alternative*	A	B	C	Most polluting alternative*	A	B
Weighted, normalised impact value for emissions	0.480	0.482	B	0.364	0.368	0.498	B	75.9	76.3
... for energy impacts	0.097	0.113	B	0.090	0.105	0.100	B	92.6	92.6
... for resource consumption	0.100	0.085	A	0.093	0.078	0.091	A	92.6	92.6
... for land use	0.005	0.005	identical characteristic	0.004	0.004	0.004	identical characteristic	92.6	92.6
... for toxicity potential	0.200	0.165	A	0.097	0.087	0.200	A	48.7	52.6
... for risk potential	0.071	0.100	B	0.040	0.050	0.100	B	56.0	50.0
Total ecological impact	*0.953*	*0.950*	*A*	*0.689*	*0.693*	*0.993*	*B*	*72.2*	*72.9*

* Only alternatives A and B are considered

Dyckhoff et al. (2015b) have analysed the source of the violation and the necessary adjustments to avoid that shortcoming. It is the *range effect* that can be accounted for the cause of such violations in multi-attributive evaluations (Eisenführ et al. 2010, pp.154, 385f.). To neutralise the range effect, changes in the range of the consequences (e.g. when alternatives are modified, included or eliminated) should result in clearly prescribed adjustments of the attributes' weights. The general logic behind the correct adjustment of weights is that the weight attached needs to be decreased (increased) for a narrower (broader) range of the respective criterion.[5]

Example 4.7 (4.6 continued): Results of EEA with adjusted weights

Looking at the data in Table 4.3, the inclusion of alternative C results in a broader range for nine ecological criteria: e.g. for GWP, the former worst value of 2,958,240 units of alternative B is amplified to 3,804,116 units of alternative C. The last two columns in Table 4.4 represent the relative shift in the impact categories after inserting alternative C. On the one hand, the impact categories without variation of the range (energy impacts, resource consumption and land use) are identically reduced for the alternatives by 92.6 % of the original value. On the other hand, the weights of the impact categories with variation of the range (all others) do not neutralise the range effect thus causing a modified relative valuation of the alternatives in the subcategories and the resulting total ecological impact.[6] A change of the preference order for the sub-criteria is generally possible but does not occur in this example. However, the relative changes have an impact when aggregated: as noted before, the preference order changes at the

---

[5] "This is due to the fact that for the small interval, the value difference between the worst and best attribute levels is larger than the value difference that we obtain for the same attribute levels in the extended interval (with a re-normalised value function)" (Eisenführ et al. 2010, p. 151).

[6] Please note that the ranges of further sub-criteria also do not change, but due to varying ranges of other sub-criteria of the same category, the corresponding final aggregated criteria ranges for *Emissions*, *Toxicity potential* and *Risk potential* do change.

third and last aggregation stage. What should be noted at this point is that, obviously, the range effect is the cause of the reversal of the preference order.

The last column of Table 4.5 displays the weights, which the EEA should use for a correct compensation of the range effect while the prior two columns show the weights used in the current procedure in both samples. From the inconsistencies it becomes clear that there is no aggregation stage with a correct compensation. To avoid the influence of the range effect and a potential violation of the principle of independence from irrelevant alternatives, the weights have to be adjusted as explained above. For example, EEA uses 46.8 % as (normalized) weight for GWP in sample 2 instead of 48.3 % as correct one.

Table 4.6 shows that after an according adjustment of all weights in the EEA, i.e. applying the weights from the last column in Table 4.5 for sample 2, there are consistent results regarding the preference order in samples 1 and 2. Here, the reconstruction of the preference order holds for both the total impact aggregation and its preparation stages. The influence of the range effect is neutralised by the consistent adjustment of the weights, and the potential violation of the rationality principle is prevented.

Table 4.5 EEA weights versus correctly adjusted weights (cf. Dyckhoff et al. 2015b, Table 3)

Aggregation step	Sample / Criteria	Normalised weight in S1 – acc. to EEA [%]	Normalised weight in S2 – acc. to EEA [%]	Normalised weight in S2 – adjusted [%]
1	GWP	44.4	46.8	48.3
	ODP	0.1	0.7	3.0
	POCP	26.9	25.0	22.8
	AP	28.5	27.5	25.9
2	Emissions to air	31.1	27.6	21.6
	Emissions to water	2.9	10.4	30.9
	Emissions to soil	66.0	62.0	47.5
3	Emissions	48.2	49.8	43.9
	Energy impacts	11.3	10.5	5.9
	Resource consumption	10.0	9.3	5.2
	Land use	0.5	0.4	0.2
	Toxicity potential	20.0	20.0	34.3
	Risk potential	10.0	10.0	10.4
Weights for aggregation of the life cycle phases: Toxicity potential	Production	20.0	20.0	13.8
	Utilisation	50.0	50.0	77.0
	Deposit/disposal	30.0	30.0	9.1
Weights for aggregation of the life cycle phases: Risk potential	Pollution by traffic	30.0	30.0	21.4
	Uncertainty of decline	40.0	40.0	57.1
	Burden of change to the status quo	30.0	30.0	21.4

Without going into much further details, the example demonstrates that the EEA method (as far as described in the literature) violates a well-founded rationality axiom. The range effect is accounted for the cause of this violation.[7] Dyckhoff et al.

---

[7] In particular, the weights for the attributes *Toxicity potential* and *Risk potential* are assessed globally instead of being assessed subject to the ranges; and for the remaining attributes, the pivotal

(2015b) have shown how to avoid this fault by adjusting the weights when including or eliminating alternatives. Thus, undesired changes in the relation of the preference scores and moreover also in the resulting preference order cannot occur.

Table 4.6 EEA results for consistent weights (cf. Dyckhoff et al. 2015b, Table 4)

Alternatives / Criteria	Sample 1 (S1)			Sample 2 (S2) without range effect				S2/S1 [%]	
	A	B	Most polluting alternative*	A	B	C	Most polluting alternative*	A	B
Weighted, normalised impact value for emissions	0.480	0.482	B	0.251	0.252	0.439	B	52.2	52.2
... for energy impacts	0.097	0.113	B	0.051	0.059	0.056	B	52.2	52.2
... for resource consumption	0.100	0.085	B	0.052	0.044	0.051	B	52.2	52.2
... for land use	0.005	0.005	identical characteristic	0.002	0.002	0.002	identical characteristic	52.2	52.2
... for toxicity potential	0.200	0.165	A	0.104	0.086	0.343	A	52.2	52.2
... for risk potential	0.071	0.100	B	0.037	0.052	0.104	B	52.2	52.2
Total ecological impact	*0.953*	*0.950*	*A*	*0.498*	*0.496*	*0.996*	*A*	*52.2*	*52.2*

* Only alternatives A and B are considered

Regarding the determination of the alternatives in an EEA, it is recommended to include "as many alternatives in the marketplace or in development as possible that can perform the same function" (Uhlman and Saling 2010, p. 18). The compilation of the set of alternatives is crucial for the analysis and its results (Dyckhoff and Ahn 1998). Usually, the set should include 'like with like' alternatives, but sometimes 'apples and oranges' are evaluated. Such outliers may appear when similar alternatives are compared to the alternative of maintaining a status-quo, e.g. when comparing the use of pesticides to conventional cultivation. In particular, if the status-quo alternative is irrelevant in the sense that it is worse in all the criteria considered than any other alternative, it must be ensured that this outlier is not relevant in the sense that it influences the preference between the other alternatives. Such an influence might appear inadvertently. However, as a general problem in the LCA context, the model parameters provide scope for manipulation (Wenzel 1998, p. 286) – at least if the process is intransparent: Then, by adding or leaving out an outlier alternative, the analysis may produce a result within the ranking of the other alternatives which is preferred for some 'political' reasons of the decision maker or some interested party.

There seems to exist no better applied methodology of EEA than that of BASF. Its improvement by Dyckhoff et al. (2015b) intends to avoid manipulation possibilities by obeying well established rationality requirements. Ultimately, rationality represents an underlying requirement of any performance evaluation conception and tools in practice. "The fact that intuitive behaviour so often violates the most basic

---

problem is the combination of relevance factors with societal factors as the latter are constant for all EEA studies (though periodically updated) without considering individual ranges and therefore enabling the range effect.

rationality principles increases the relevance of decision analysis for all people eager to obey the rules of rationality" (Eisenführ et al. 2010, p. 9). In particular, a foundation augmented by decision theory – and perhaps also by multi-criteria production theory (MCPT; cf. Sect. 3.5) – will be fruitful not only for the EEA method of BASF but for all methods of ecological performance measurement and LCA. Respective methods must compromise between comprehensible and non-ambiguous results on the one hand and the rising influence of subjective value judgements that comes with an increasing aggregation level on the other hand.

4.4 Detection of Key Performance Indicators and Their Dependencies

The relationship between the inputs and outputs of an activity at the one end and the fundamental goals of a performance evaluation at the other is often complex, and it is difficult to untangle the chain of effects on the relevant objectives (cf. Sect. 3.5, in particular Fig. 3.4, regarding sustainability). In order to derive a hierarchy of corresponding value functions – connecting the inputs and outputs of the activity of a decision-making unit (DMU) with the key performance indicators (KPIs) of the highest level in a quantitative manner –, it is at first necessary to determine the various relevant KPIs of the different value levels of such a hierarchical system of objectives (i.e. costs and benefits in the terminology of MCPT in Chapter 2). In prescriptive decision theory, different requirements for such systems are considered. They include the wide-spread elimination of means/objectives-relationships within the specified decision or evaluation context (in favour of the fundamentality of objectives) as well as completeness, simplicity, no redundancy, measurability, and preference independence (Keeney 1992, p. 82; Eisenführ et al. 2010, Sect. 3.4). However, fully satisfying all these requirements remains mostly a utopia, as they are rarely compatible. Nevertheless, they should be taken into account to an adequate extent, even if limitations of accuracy are unavoidable for reasons of practicality. As a good compromise the framework of the ***Balanced Scorecard*** (BSC) may be useful, which has been developed by Kaplan and Norton (1996) for the strategic management of firms (cf. Biazzo and Garengo 2012).

Dyckhoff et al. (2011) have constructed a BSC based methodology for the transparent and systematic development of industry-wide solutions for main types of strategic KPI systems. Such a development faces a dilemma as there is a gap between abstraction on the one hand and the adjustment in individual cases with minimal effort on the other hand. Therefore, they developed generic types of strategic performance measurement systems exemplarily for the waste management industry.

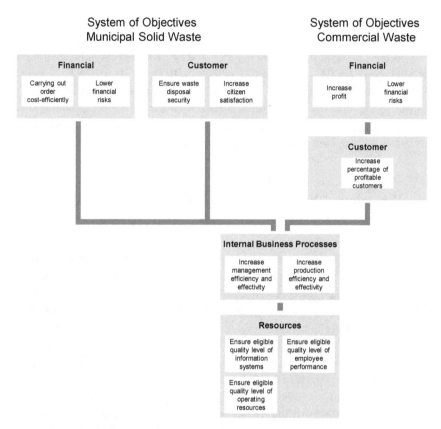

Fig. 4.4 Two generic systems of objectives for waste management (cf. Dyckhoff et al. 2011, Fig. 4)

This was done both according to inductive-empirical *case study methodology* following Yin (2003) and in a deductive-analytical way drawing on existing theoretical and methodological knowledge of decision analysis and performance management in accordance with the ***Design Science Research Methodology***, in particular the frameworks of Hevner et al. (2004) and Peffers et al. (2008).

Implementing a BSC ideally comprises at least the determination of strategic objectives within a perspective hierarchy, their connection by means of cause/effect-chains, and the selection of appropriate indicators (Ahn 2001). The perspective hierarchy helps to identify dependencies between the objectives faster and to define their priorities in an appropriate way. In the cases of waste management companies, studied by Dyckhoff et al. (2011), six basic firm types with corresponding KPI systems emerged. One criterion of typification is the strategic orientation of handling *municipal solid waste versus commercial waste*. It shows significant differences for both public and private firms which require a differentiated need for indicators and

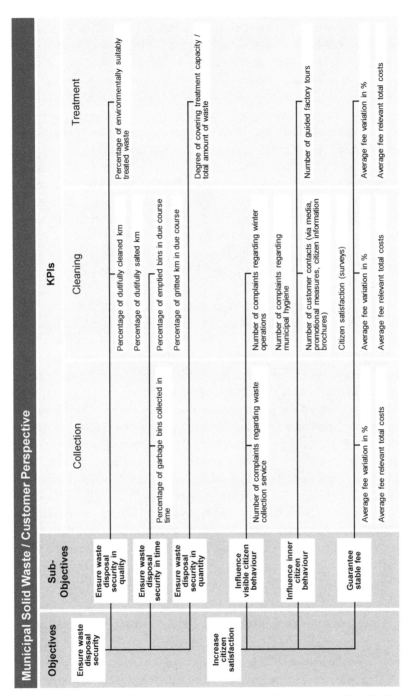

Fig. 4.5 Objectives and KPIs of customer perspective for municipal solid waste (Dyckhoff et al. 2011, Fig. 5)

induce the two generic objectives systems of Figure 4.4. They only differ in terms of the *financial* and *customer perspective* for these two kinds of waste (left versus right in Fig. 4.4). The second criterion is relevant for the KPIs of lower levels, only, and consists of *collection, cleaning and recycling* as three main disposal areas (cf. Fig. 4.5).

Figure 4.4 contains twelve generic top objectives in total, spreading relatively evenly between the four BSC perspectives for the two different types of waste. The type-specific splitting of the BSC perspectives 'financial' and 'customer' is necessary due to the very different strategic orientation of municipal versus commercial waste management companies (empirically found by the conducted case studies). Furthermore, in case of the municipal solid waste management, the conventional linear BSC hierarchy is adapted so that the financial and the customer perspective are based equally on the top level. For the other two perspectives, i.e. the internal business process perspective and the resource perspective, however, there is no need for any kind of differentiation of the associated five generic top objectives between the two types of waste.

For each of the type-specific BSC perspectives, Dyckhoff et al. (2011) present prototypical KPI systems such that the 12 primary objectives become concrete in a system comprising a total of 23 subobjectives and 117 KPIs. As an example, Figure 4.5 shows such a system of objectives and KPIs for the customer perspective of municipal solid waste management firms, differentiated according to the three main disposal areas (i.e. collection, cleaning, treatment).

The above sketched systems of generic objectives and KPIs for waste management firms are based on existing approaches both from theory and practice and are evaluated by experts and prospective users. They are enhanced or improved to an industry-wide concept by following a systematic procedure in accordance with Design Science Research Methodology which is also useful for other industries and thus may reduce the dissatisfaction in the respective industry complaining about the lack of balanced performance measurement systems. However, even if such a hierarchical system of objectives and KPIs can be derived in a concrete instance, it is to be questioned whether quantitative functional dependencies between the objectives and indicators of different hierarchical levels can be found or even exist.

4.5   Comprehensive Concepts of Performance Evaluation

Chapter 3 has shown that DEA is a powerful tool for applications where the evaluated DMUs are described by activities representing real processes which generate products or services and are based on a convex or even linear technology, and where the performance indicators depend linearly on inputs and outputs. Nevertheless, after forty years of research since the pioneering article of Charnes et al. (1978) with thousands of application-oriented scientific papers, empirical evidence that DEA has really improved the practice of performance measurement and benchmarking in real-life non-production contexts is rare. The main reason for this deficit may be that DEA is founded on concepts of production theory such as production possibility set or returns to scale. These concepts can hardly be applied to pure multiple-criteria evaluation problems, which are often attempted to be solved using DEA.

Against this background, Wojcik et al. (2019) have systematically investigated strengths and weaknesses of DEA in the exemplary case of welfare evaluation using real data on 27 countries of the European Union. They analyse and explain the differences in the results of various frequently used DEA models for two different, but strongly connected sets of welfare indicators, thereby demonstrating the pitfalls, which often arise in the application of DEA, as well as some approaches for avoiding them. Despite the exemplary nature of their investigation, the conclusions for this specific application field can be viewed as characteristic for other non-production contexts, too.

Thus, it is necessary to raise more awareness for the distinct performance and benchmarking results that may be obtained when applying different variants of DEA models and when modifying the selected inputs and outputs. Otherwise, however, serious doubts can be cast on the proposition that DEA can really "be viewed as a multiple-criteria evaluation methodology" (Cook et al. 2014, p. 2) that is in general appropriate to derive resilient information for benchmarking the performance of DMUs. At least, some further reflections and a solid reasoning for applying DEA are necessary so that its results can be accepted as valid. To the best of our knowledge, such reflections are rare in the DEA literature (cf. Dyson et al. 2001 for some general remarks on pitfalls and protocols).

Facing the difficulties and advantages as well as disadvantages of certain DEA model choices, extended and more detailed frameworks could be helpful to guide the user through a well-founded selection of indicators as well as through the reasonable choice of proper DEA model characteristics. They should persuade the user to adequately consider all necessary questions, which is why such frameworks should be systematically and iteratively designed. Although there are already some useful and supportive works on frameworks for DEA (see e.g. Emrouznejad and De Witte 2010), their validity still has to be successfully approved in practice. Moreover, such frameworks need to be further developed continuously to meet the requirements of all different types of DEA applications. Particularly, adopting the generalised perspective on DEA based on multi-criteria production theory (MCPT), as described in Chapters 2 and 3, may provide some more valuable advices for the further enhancement of such frameworks (see Wojcik 2018 for such an approach). This is especially true regarding more detailed insights for the systematic derivation and justification of performance indicators (cf. Sect. 4.4), a topic which has not been discussed sufficiently in the DEA literature so far. Thus, under certain circumstances, the application of DEA in instances which are not directly based on a classical production process can either be facilitated and enhanced or otherwise be avoided.

A main conclusion of the *foundations for performance evaluation* analysed in this book is therefore that the prerequisites to apply quantitative methods of performance measurement *in practice* – like e.g. DEA or eco-efficiency analysis – are usually very *challenging*. Though, there is a strong need for such approaches which often is pointedly said by the phrase: *"You can't manage what you can't measure!"* However, this assertion has to be contrasted with a second well-known phrase which states: *"What you measure is what you get!"* It points out to the severe neglection of those performance criteria which are not measurable in valid quantitative terms although of high relevance. In order to avoid such a dilemma, any convincing performance evaluation should in fact use all relevant valid information, regardless of which quality. Hence, *performance evaluation is more than a pure measurement*, even though the latter has been the focal point of this book. Nevertheless, *performance evaluation comprises performance measurement* as far as possible. Well-proven quantitative methods should be applied if the prerequisites are fulfilled, even if for parts of the data only. Their results may constitute a *management dashboard* as core of a *performance measurement and management system* (PMS; cf. Biazzo and Garengo 2012, p. 2). But it should be given no more credit than to the other (qualitative) valid performance data. *Informed peer reviews* form a good compromise of integrating performance measurement into a comprehensive performance evaluation if quantitative and qualitative data have to be considered to obtain valid, convincing results.

References

Afsharian M, Ahn H, Neumann L (2016) Generalized DEA: An approach for supporting input/output factor determination in DEA. Benchmarking: An International Journal 23:1892–1909
Ahn H (2001) Applying the Balanced Scorecard concept: An experience report. Long Range Planning 34:441–461
Ahn H, Le MH (2014) An insight into the specification of the input-output set for DEA-based bank efficiency measurement. Management Review Quarterly 64:3–37
Ahn H, Le MH (2016) Decision-oriented performance measurement framework. In: Ahn H, Clermont M, Souren R (ed) Nachhaltiges Entscheiden – Beiträge zum multiperspektivischen Performancemanagement von Wertschöpfungsprozessen. Springer Gabler, Wiesbaden, pp 369–383
Belton V, Stewart TJ (1999) DEA and MCDA – Competing or complementary approaches? In: Meskens N, Roubens M (ed) Advances in Decision Analysis. Springer, Dordrecht, pp 87–103

Biazzo S, Garengo P (2012) Performance Measurement with the Balanced Scorecard: A Practical Approach to Implementation within SMEs. SpringerBriefs in Business 6, Berlin/Heidelberg

Charnes A, Cooper WW, Rhodes E (1978) Measuring efficiency of decision making units. European Journal of Operational Research 2:429–444

Cook WD, Zhu J (2007) Classifying inputs and outputs in Data Envelopment Analysis. European Journal of Operational Research 180:692–699

Cook WD, Tone K, Zhu J (2014) Data envelopment analysis: Prior to choosing a model. Omega 44:1–4

Dyckhoff H, Ahn H (1998) Integrierte Alternativengenerierung und -bewertung. Die Betriebswirtschaft 58:49–63

Dyckhoff H, Gutgesell S (2015) Properties of DEA-integrated balance and specialization measures. OR Spectrum 37:503–527

Dyckhoff H, Souren R, Elyas A (2011) Reference data models for the strategic controlling of waste management firms: A new methodology for industry solution design. Business & Information Systems Engineering 3:65–75

Dyckhoff H, Clermont M, Dirksen A, Mbock E (2013) Measuring balanced effectiveness and efficiency of German business schools' research performance. In: Dilger A, Dyckhoff H, Fandel G (ed) Performance Management im Hochschulbereich. Springer Gabler, Wiesbaden, pp 39–60

Dyckhoff H, Mbock E, Gutgesell S (2015a) Distance-based measures of specialization and balance in multi-criteria: A DEA-integrated method. Journal of Multi-Criteria Decision Analysis 22:197–212

Dyckhoff H, Quandel A, Waletzke K (2015b) Rationality of eco-efficiency methods: Is the BASF analysis dependent on irrelevant alternatives? International Journal of Life Cycle Assessment 20:1557–1567

Dyson RG, Allen R, Camanho AS, Podinovski VV, Sarrico CC, Shale EA (2001) Pitfalls and protocols in DEA. European Journal of Operational Research 132:245–259

Eisenführ F, Weber M, Langer T (2010) Rational Decision Making. Springer, Berlin et al.

Emrouznejad A, De Witte K (2010) COOPER-framework: A unified process for non-parametric projects. European Journal of Operational Research 207:1573–1586

Hevner AR, March ST, Park J, Ram S (2004) Design science in information science research. MIS Quarterly 28:75–105

Kaplan RS, Norton DP (1996) The Balanced Scorecard: Translating Strategy into Action. Harvard, Cambridge

Keeney RL (1992) Value-Focused Thinking: A Path to Creative Decisionmaking. Harvard, Cambridge

Kleine A, Saling P, von Hauff M (2004) Ökoeffizienz-Analyse zu Entsorgungsoptionen Mineralölkohlenwasserstoff-kontaminierter Böden – Bodenbehandlung oder Deponierung? Mainz

Peffers K, Tuunanen T, Rothenberger MA, Chatterjee S (2008) A design science research methodology for information systems research. Journal of Management Information Systems 24:45–77

Saling P (2016) The BASF Eco-Efficiency Analysis: A 20-year Success Story. BASF SE, Ludwigshafen

Saling P, Kicherer A, Dittrich-Krämer B, Wittlinger R, Zombik W, Schmidt I, Schrott W, Schmidt S (2002) Eco-efficiency Analysis by BASF: The Method. International Journal of Life Cycle Assessment 7:203–218

Seiford LM, Zhu J (2002) Modeling undesirable factors in efficiency evaluation. European Journal of Operational Research 142:16–20

Souren R (1996a) Theorie betrieblicher Reduktion. Physica, Heidelberg

Souren R (1996b) Analyse, Planung und Steuerung stofflicher Reduktionsprozesse bei inhomogener Abfallqualität. Umweltwirtschaftsforum 4(4):13–19

Uhlman BW, Saling P (2010) Measuring and Communicating Sustainability through Eco-Efficiency Analysis. In: CEP December 2010 (special expanded web-only version), American Institute of Chemical Engineers, CEP magazine article, December 2010:17–26d

Uhlman BW, Saling P (2017) The BASF eco-efficiency toolbox: Holistic evaluation of sustainable solutions. In: Abraham M (ed) Encyclopedia of Sustainable Technologies, vol 1. Elsevier, Amsterdam, pp 131–144

Wagner JM, Shimshak DG (2007) Stepwise selection of variables in data envelopment analysis: Procedures and managerial perspectives. European Journal of Operational Research 180:57–67

Wenzel H (1998) Application dependency of LCA methodology: Key variable and their mode of influencing the method. International Journal of Life Cycle Assessment 3:281–288

Wojcik V (2018) Performanceanalyse mittels Verallgemeinerter Data Envelopment Analysis: Vorgehensmodell und Evaluation. Dr. Kovač, Hamburg

Wojcik V, Dyckhoff H, Gutgesell S (2017) The desirable input of undesirable factors in Data Envelopment Analysis. Annals of Operations Research 259:461–484

Wojcik V, Dyckhoff H, Clermont M (2019) Is data envelopment analysis a suitable tool for performance measurement and benchmarking in non-production contexts? Business Research 12 (2): 559–595 (DOI 10.1007/s40685-018-0077-z; open access)

Yin RK (2003) Case Study Research: Design and Methods. 3rd ed, Sage, Thousand Oaks

CPSIA information can be obtained
at www.ICGtesting.com
Printed in the USA
LVHW081932170120
644013LV00002B/13